state of world population 2009

Facing a changing world:
women, population and climate

Copyright © UNFPA 2009

United Nations Population Fund
Thoraya Ahmed Obaid, Executive Director

state of world population 2009

12/09

 1   2

How do population dynamics affect greenhouse gases and climate change? Will urbanization and an ageing population help or hinder efforts to adapt to a warming world? What's the best way to protect humanity from extreme weather and rising seas? And could better access to reproductive health care and improved relations between men and women make a critical difference in addressing the challenge of climate change? The answers to these questions are found in *The State of World Population 2009.*

© Joerg Boethling/Still Pictures

state of world population 2009
Facing a changing world:
women, population and climate

Background image: © Ed Darack/Science Faction/Corbis

Foreword

When climate negotiators gather in Copenhagen in December for the 15th Conference of Parties to the United Nations Framework Convention on Climate Change, they will be setting a course that will move the world's governments either forward or merely sideways in tackling one of the most challenging problems human beings have ever faced: how to manage our influence on climate and how to adapt to climate change now and well into the future.

Many of the discussions in the lead-up to Copenhagen revolved around the relative responsibilities of countries for limiting the growth of greenhouse-gas emissions and for funding efforts to shift to low-carbon energy and other technologies.

What's the best approach for reducing carbon emissions? Who should shoulder the financial responsibility for addressing current and future climate change?

These questions are critically important. But also important are fundamental questions about how climate change will affect women, men, boys and girls around the world, and indeed within nations, and how individual behaviour can undermine or contribute to the global effort to address climate change. The poor, particularly in developing countries, are likely to face the worst effects of a changing climate. The poor are more likely to live in areas vulnerable to floods, storms and rising seas. And they are more likely to depend on agriculture and fishing for a living and therefore risk going hungry or losing their livelihoods when droughts strike, rains become unpredictable and hurricanes move with unprecedented force. And among the poor, women are especially vulnerable.

In addition to the ongoing discussion on technical and financial aspects, the climate debate of the future must be further enriched by taking into account the human dimensions, including gender, that suffuse every facet of the problem. A Copenhagen agreement that helps people to reduce greenhouse-gas emissions and adapt to climate change by harnessing the insight and creativity of women and men would launch a genuinely effective long-term global strategy to deal with climate change.

UNFPA, the United Nations Population Fund, is a development agency that promotes the right of every woman, man and child to enjoy a life of health and equal opportunity and helps reduce poverty. UNFPA helps ensure that every pregnancy is wanted, every birth is safe, every young person is free of HIV and AIDS and every girl and woman is treated with dignity and respect. The causes we champion are also causes that are relevant to climate change.

This 2009 edition of *The State of World Population* shows that climate change is more than an issue of energy efficiency or industrial carbon emissions; it is also an issue of population dynamics, poverty and gender equity.

Over the years, the international community's approach to population policies has evolved from a top-down focus on demographic change to a people-centred approach based on human rights and informed choice. Voices that invoke "population control" as a response to climate change fail to grasp the complexity of the issue and ignore international consensus. Governments agreed at the 1994 International Conference on Population and Development that human rights and gender equality should guide all population and development-related programmes, including those aimed at protecting the environment. This begins with upholding the right of women and couples to determine the number and spacing of their children, and creating or expanding opportunities and choices for women and girls, allowing them to fully participate in their societies and contribute to economic growth and development.

Climate change is partly the result of an approach to development and economic growth that has proven to be unsustainable. Halting climate change requires a fresh, more equitable and sustainable approach to the way we live, produce and consume. Reining in the run-away greenhouse effect responsible for extreme weather and rising seas may therefore require a new definition of "progress" and a new development paradigm.

The complexity of the challenge of reducing greenhouse-gas emissions and adapting to climate change requires us to look beyond the obvious and to marshal innovative strategies. The most effective solutions to climate change, however, will be those that come from the bottom up, that are based on communities' knowledge of their immediate environment, that empower—not victimize or overburden—those who must adapt to a new world, and that do not create a new dependency relationship between developed and developing countries. The only lasting solution will be one that puts people at its centre.

This report shows that women have the power to mobilize against climate change, but this potential can be realized only through policies that empower them. It also shows the required support that would allow women to fully contribute to adaptation, mitigation and building resilience to climate change.

By taking a broader, more nuanced approach to climate change that factors in gender and population, the governments of the world, and indeed civil society and we ourselves in the United Nations, will make a valuable contribution to the Copenhagen conference and meaningful action in addressing this long-term challenge.

Thoraya Ahmed Obaid
Executive Director, UNFPA

Overview

"We have read the science. Global warming is real, and we are a prime cause. . . .
We must set an agenda—create a roadmap to the future, coupled with a timeline that produces
a deal by 2009. In this, it helps to have a vision of how the future might look if we succeed."

—BAN Ki-moon[1]

Climate—the average of weather over time—is always changing, but never in known human experience more dramatically than it is likely to change in the coming century. For millennia, since civilizations arose from ancient farming societies, the earth's climate as a whole was relatively stable, with temperatures and patterns of rainfall that have supported human life and its expansion around the globe.

A growing body of evidence shows that recent climate change is primarily the result of human activity. The influence of human activity on climate change is complex. It is about what we consume, the types of energy we produce and use, whether we live in a city or on a farm, whether we live in a rich or poor country, whether we are young or old, what we eat, and even the extent to which women and men enjoy equal rights and opportunities. It is also about our growing numbers—approaching 7 billion. As the growth of population, economies and consumption outpaces the earth's capacity to adjust, climate change could become much more extreme—and conceivably catastrophic. Population dynamics tell one part of a larger, more intricate story about the way some countries and people have pursued development and defined progress and about how others have had little say in the decisions that affect their lives.

Climate change's influence on people is also complex, spurring migration, destroying livelihoods, disrupting economies, undermining development and exacerbating inequities between the sexes.

Climate change is about people.

People cause climate change. People are affected by it. People need to adapt to it. And only people have the power to stop it.

Not all people or countries, however, are created equal when it comes to the greenhouse-gas emissions that are warming our atmosphere. Until now, the industrialized countries generated the lion's share of climate-altering carbon and other gases but have been relatively immune to the effects of climate change. The developing world has been responsible for a smaller share of greenhouse-gas emissions yet is already having to shoulder more of the burden for coping with and adapting to extreme weather events, rising sea levels, floods and drought. The industrialized countries created most of the problem, but the world's poor will face the biggest problems in adapting to it. And, if the world is to avoid dangerous climate change, there may be little room left in the atmosphere for poor countries to develop economically through the same carbon-intensive energy patterns the industrialized countries relied upon in their own development over the last two centuries.

What is climate change?

The earth's surface is warming. The temperature increase since the late 1800s may seem small—0.74 degrees Celsius—but the impact on people is likely to be profound. The impact will be even greater as temperatures continue rising, by as much as 6.4 degrees Celsius by 2100.

◀ *Digging for snails in a dried lake bed in Thailand.*
© Werachai Wansamngan/UNEP/Still Pictures

On the icy slopes and plains leading down from the Huayna Potosi and Chacaltaya mountains lies a string of tiny communities that eke out a living by keeping llamas, sheep and chickens and growing small crops of potatoes and *oca*, a perennial plant grown in the central and southern Andes. In some parts, the slopes they cultivate are so steep that farming seems like a gravity-defying act.

The glaciers that used to provide generous amounts of crystal clear water to the communities have shrunk dramatically over the past 15 to 20 years, affecting people in large and small ways—from the disruption of water supplies for urban centres like the sprawling and poor city of El Alto and Bolivia's capital, La Paz, to the closure of the ski slopes of Chacaltaya, a glacier now reduced to a small chunk of snow and ice nestled just below the 18,000-foot summit.

Nearly all of the world's so-called tropical glaciers are located in the Andes. About 20 per cent of them are in Bolivia.

According to Bolivia's Ministry of Water and the Environment, glaciers in the country's Cordillera Real diminished by 84 square kilometres, or 24 per cent, between 1987 and 2004, and the disintegration continues.

Leucadia Quispe, born and raised in the Botijlaca community in the foothills of both Chacaltaya and Huayna Potosi, is just one of many Bolivians affected by this environmental crisis. Leucadia grows potatoes and oca in what must be one of the harshest climates in South America. She is 60 years old and has eight children, only one of whom remains in Botijlaca. The other seven have migrated to other parts of the country, "because there is no way to make a living here."

Every day she wakes up at 4 a.m. and boils water to make chamomile tea. Breakfast is *caya*—oca that has been soaked in water wells for two months. For lunch, the family eats oca, potatoes and sometimes llama meat or mutton.

She says the family has to carry water from the river for their own use as well as for irrigation of their crops. "There is less water now," she says. "We used to be able to get water for irrigation from the streams that came down from the Huayna Potosi glacier, but the

Leucadia Quispe harvests oca on her tiny plot in rural Botijlaca, Bolivia. She says there is less water for irrigation every year.
© Trygve Olfarnes/UNFPA

streams are no longer there, so now we have to collect water from a river farther up in the valley."

She now spends hours hauling water in five-litre containers, one in each hand. The dwindling water supply also results in less fodder for her llamas and sheep, and some of her llamas have already starved to death, she says.

As temperatures rise, weather patterns shift with potentially catastrophic consequences, especially for the world's poor.

A rapid and large build-up of greenhouse gases in the earth's atmosphere is almost certainly to blame for most or all the temperature increase. The most common greenhouse gas is carbon dioxide, with methane a close second. Such greenhouse gases occur naturally and serve to retain some of the sun's warmth. Without a "greenhouse effect," the earth's surface would be too cold to sustain life. But because the greenhouse gases that are naturally in the atmosphere have been augmented by those resulting from human activity, the equilibrium that keeps the earth at a relatively constant temperature has been disrupted. Since the Industrial Revolution, intense burning of wood, charcoal, coal, oil, and gas has resulted in increased concentrations of carbon dioxide in the atmosphere. Rice-growing, livestock-raising, and burning organic wastes have more than doubled methane concentrations. The use of artificial fertilizers, made possible by techniques developed in the early 20th century, has released large amounts of another greenhouse gas, nitrous oxide, into air and water. And since the 1920s, industry has used a number of man-made carbon compounds for refrigeration and fire suppression. Some of these compounds have been found to be very powerful greenhouse gases.

Future climate change will depend largely on how fast greenhouse gases accumulate in the atmosphere. That in turn will depend on how much is emitted and on how much nature is able to absorb. Since 2000, "anthropogenic" or human-caused carbon-dioxide emissions have been increasing four times faster than in the previous decade. Most of the emissions came from burning fossil fuels.[2]

At the same time, natural carbon "sinks" that absorb some of our emissions are unable to perform this function with their former efficiency. The main carbon sinks are the oceans, frozen tracts in the Arctic, and forests, all of which are losing their capacity to absorb greenhouse gases from the atmosphere.

Impact

Climate change has the potential to reverse the hard-earned development gains of the past decades and the progress toward achieving the Millennium Development Goals, according to the World Bank.[3] Setbacks will result from water scarcities, intense tropical storms and storm surges, floods, loss of glacial meltwater for irrigated agriculture, food shortages and health crises.

Climate change threatens to worsen poverty or burden marginalized and vulnerable groups with additional hardships. In Southeast Asia, for example, about 221 million people already live below the $2-a-day poverty line.[4] Many of the region's poor live in coastal areas and in low-lying deltas, and many of these poor people are smallholder farmers or people who earn their living from the seas. Poor households are especially vulnerable to climate change because their marginal income provides little or no access to health services or other safety nets to protect against the threats from changing conditions and because they lack the resources to relocate when crises strike. Some of the possible direct threats that climate change could pose on the region's poor include death and illness resulting from extreme heat, unusual cold, infectious diseases and malnutrition.

Also as a result of climate change, sea levels will rise, threatening low-lying, densely populated coastal areas and small island states. Indonesia, for example, could lose as many as 2,000 small islands by 2030 as a result of rising seas.[5]

 2 WOMEN TAKE THE BRUNT OF CLIMATE CHANGE

Filipina farmer Trinidad Domingo views the coming rice harvest season with trepidation. A typhoon destroyed much of her crop, and Domingo estimates that her two-hectare plot will produce less than the usual 200 sacks of rice.

Typhoons are a part of life for most Filipino farmers but they know how to minimize losses brought on by heavy rains. Domingo starts tilling rice as early as June and July—the start of the wet season. By planting early, she can avoid most rain damage. But this year, Domingo couldn't plant until August, as the wet season started late.

"This is really a problem for me as I invested a lot of money, about PhP 60,000 ($1,250), for this cropping season. I may not be able to repay my loan and my family may really need to tighten belts," she said. Domingo heads an extended family that includes siblings and their numerous children.

A lean rice harvest threatens her family's food security. She is also hard pressed to find the money to repay loans and buy other necessities.

Erratic weather events are causing problems for farmers like Domingo. The increased frequency of heat waves, floods and drought are believed to have drastically reduced both agricultural and fishery output, and raised food prices.

This, in turn, increases the burden for women and girls, as they are the ones expected to ensure that there is enough food for the family, according to Ines Smyth, Gender Advisor of Oxfam in the United Kingdom.

Speaking at a conference in Manila in October on gender and climate change, Smyth noted that owing to higher food prices, "women substitute time for cash. They take on extra work, even if they're poorly paid." The four-day conference was organized by the Centre for Asia-Pacific Women in Politics and the United Nations International Strategy for Disaster Risk Reduction.

In coastal areas, among the fishing communities of the Philippines, women are now grappling with the harsh impact of climate change, according to a report presented by the Centre for Empowerment and Resource Development, Inc. (CERD), a Manila-based non-governmental organization that implements community-based coastal resource management.

"The decline in fish catch puts additional burden on the women. Aside from their household chores and participation in fishing activity, they have to find additional sources of income like working as domestic helpers for more affluent families," CERD's project development officer, Marita P. Rodriguez, said.

By Prime Sarmiento. Excerpts reprinted with permission from the Inter Press News Agency, October 2008.

Climate change will not only endanger lives and undermine livelihoods, but it threatens to exacerbate the gaps between rich and poor and amplify the inequities between women and men.

Women—particularly those in poor countries—will be affected differently than men. They are among the most vulnerable to climate change, partly because in many countries they make up the larger share of the agricultural work force and partly because they tend to have access to fewer income-earning opportunities. Women manage households and care for family members, which often limits their mobility and increases their vulnerability to sudden weather-related natural disasters. Drought and erratic rainfall force women to work harder to secure food, water and energy for their homes. Girls drop out of school to help their mothers with these tasks. This cycle of deprivation, poverty and inequality undermines the social capital needed to deal effectively with climate change.

Health effects

In May 2009, *The Lancet* medical journal called climate change "the biggest global health threat of the 21st century."[6] The "epidemiological outcome of climate change on disease patterns worldwide will be profound, especially

 GLOSSARY

Adaptation refers to preparing for and coping with the impacts of climate change. According to the Intergovernmental Panel on Climate Change, this term refers to changes in processes, practices, and structures to moderate potential damages or to benefit from opportunities associated with climate change.

Climate is the average of weather over time.

Climate change, for the purposes of this report, refers to the alteration of the earth's climate caused by the atmospheric accumulation of *greenhouse gases*, such as carbon dioxide, as a result of human activity. Greenhouse gases absorb solar heat and warm the earth's surface. The terms "anthropogenic," "human-induced" and "human-caused" sometimes precede "climate change," as a reminder that almost all the climate change discussed in this report is occurring or is considered likely to occur beyond natural oscillations.

Gender refers to the array of socially conditioned expectations and learned roles of how females and males in any society interact, live their lives and work. Gender extends beyond women and girls and includes men and boys and the relationships between the sexes. Gender determines what is expected, permitted and valued in a woman or a man in a determined context.

Gender equality is the concept that all humans—men and women—are free to develop their personal abilities and make choices without the limitations set by stereotypes, rigid gender roles or prejudices. Gender equality means that the different behaviours, aspirations and needs of women and men are considered, valued and favoured equally. It does not mean that women and men are the same, but rather, that their rights, responsibilities and opportunities will not depend on whether they are born male or female.[7]

Mitigation refers to tackling the causes of climate change through actions that reduce greenhouse-gas emissions or help remove gases from the atmosphere through, for example, carbon sequestration by trees and soils.

Population dynamics are the changing characteristics of the number of human beings worldwide or in any specified geographic area, including size, rate of growth, density, geographic distribution (including flows of people within countries and across borders), and age structure (relative proportions of a population in specified age groups).

Reproductive health has been defined by the World Health Organization as a state of physical, mental and social well-being in all matters relating to the reproductive system at all stages of life. Reproductive health implies that people are able to have a satisfying and safe sex life and that they have the capability to reproduce and the freedom to decide if, when and how often to do so. Implicit in this are the right of men and women to be informed and to have access to safe, effective, affordable and acceptable methods of family planning of their choice, and the right to appropriate health-care services that enable women to safely go through pregnancy and childbirth. Reproductive health care is defined as the constellation of methods, techniques, and services that contribute to reproductive health and well-being by preventing and solving reproductive health problems.[8]

Weather refers to meteorological conditions in any one place at any one time.

in developing countries, where existing vulnerabilities to poor health remain." The incidence of vector-borne diseases, for example, will increase. Millions of additional people may be affected by malaria, as rising temperatures allow disease-carrying mosquitoes to live in higher altitudes. In addition, rising temperatures are likely to generate heat-related stress, increasing short-term mortality rates from heatstroke. Also, changing rainfall and temperature over the next decades are likely to make provision of clean water and good sanitation "more complicated than it is now."

But *The Lancet* also notes that climate change will interact with population growth in ways that put "additional stress on already-weak health systems" and will exacerbate vulnerability to the adverse health effects of climate change. "The damage done to the environment by modern society is perhaps one of the most inequitable health risks of our time," *The Lancet* explains, noting that the "carbon footprint" of the poorest 1 billion people is about 3 per cent of the world's total footprint. Still, it is the poor who bear the disproportionate brunt of our changing climate.[9] "Loss of healthy life years as a result of global environmental change—including climate change—is predicted to be 500 times greater in poor African populations than in European populations."

The World Health Organization estimates that in 2000 some 150,000 excess deaths were occurring annually—in extreme heat waves, storms, or similar events—as a result of climate change that had occurred since the 1970s.[10]

Migration

"Large-scale population movement is likely to intensify as changing climate leads to the abandonment of flooded or arid and inhospitable environments," according to *The Lancet*. "The resulting mass migration will lead to many serious health problems both directly, from the various stresses of the migration process, and indirectly, from the possible civil strife that could be caused by chaotic movement of people."

Millions of people now living in low-lying coastal areas may need to leave their homes if sea levels rise as predicted by most climate-change experts. Protracted and severe droughts may drive more farmers from rural areas to cities to seek new livelihoods. Residents of urban slums in flood-prone areas may migrate to rural areas to escape

danger. And in some instances, gradual environmental degradation may erase income-earning opportunities, driving some across national boundaries.

The reasons for which people migrate or seek refuge are complex, making it hard to forecast how climate change will affect the future of migration. Climate change nonetheless seems likely to become a major force for future population movement, probably mostly through internal displacement but also to some extent through international migration.

People and climate change

The Intergovernmental Panel on Climate Change has supported the scientific conclusion that human-caused increases in concentrations of greenhouse gases in the atmosphere are very likely the cause of most of the temperature increases the world has experienced since the middle of the 20th century. The Panel consists of more than 2,000 scientists and other experts from around the world and is sponsored by the United Nations Environment Programme (UNEP) and the World Meteorological Organization.

Greenhouse gases would not be accumulating so hazardously had the number of earth's inhabitants not increased so rapidly, but remained at 300 million people, the world population of 1,000 years ago, compared with 6.8 billion today.[11] The connection between population growth and the accumulation of greenhouse gases has barely featured in the scientific and diplomatic discussions so far. One reason for this is that population growth and what, if anything, should be done about it, have long been difficult, controversial and divisive topics. The dominant responsibility for the current build-up of greenhouse gases lies with developed countries whose population growth and fertility rates, while fairly high in earlier centuries, have now mostly subsided to the point where family sizes of two or fewer children are the norm. The vast majority of the world's population growth today occurs in developing countries, whose contribution to global greenhouse-gas emissions is historically far less than those of the developed countries. However, emissions from some large developing countries are now growing rapidly as a result of their carbon-intensive industrialization and changing patterns of consumption, as well as their current demographic growth.[12]

▲ *Drought-stricken area of Kenya. Changes in rainfall patterns threaten food production in many parts of Africa and other regions.*

© AFP/Getty Images

Beyond the projections of computerized climate models and the scenarios of the future presented by the Intergovernmental Panel on Climate Change, common sense alone suggests that a continually shifting climate will stress societies and individuals, especially those already most at risk, and will exacerbate existing inequalities.

The importance of the speed and magnitude of recent population growth in boosting future greenhouse-gas emissions is well recognized among scientists, including the authors of the Intergovernmental Panel on Climate Change's reports. Slower population growth in both developed and developing countries may help ease the task of bringing global emissions into balance with the atmosphere in the long run and enabling more immediate adaptation to change already under way. The extent to which slower population growth will matter, however, depends on the future of world economic, technological and consumption trends. The role of population growth in the growth of greenhouse-gas emissions is far from the only demographic linkage salient to climate change. Household composition is one such variable that affects the amount of greenhouse gases thrust into the atmosphere. At least one study has shown that per capita energy consumption of smaller households is significantly higher than that of larger households.[13] Some evidence suggests that changes in age structure and geographic distribution—the trend toward

living in cities, for example—may affect emissions growth. Population dynamics are likely to influence greenhouse-gas emissions in the long run. In the immediate future, population dynamics will affect countries' capacities to adapt to the impacts of climate change.

Current regimes of consumption, especially in industrialized countries, already stretch the limits of sustainability. Legitimate development aspirations in less-developed regions, which already make up more than four-fifths of the world's current population, complicate this conundrum. Improved access to sexual and reproductive health, including voluntary family planning, is essential for individual welfare and accelerates the stabilization of population, according to a group of climate-change and population experts in London in June 2009.[14] Major achievements in family planning have in the past had significant impacts on slowing population growth, and slower population growth in some countries has bought more time to prepare adaptation plans for the coming impacts of climate change.

Gender: the underrepresented variable

Relations between the sexes and attention to the specific needs of each have until recently gained little attention by those charged with addressing global climate change. The word "gender" found no mention in the United Nations Framework Convention on Climate Change (UNFCCC). However, after generally omitting gender in treaty language and international deliberations, the UNFCCC's secretariat in December 2008 formally recognized at the 14th Conference of the Parties in Poznań, Poland: "the gender dimension of climate change and its impacts are likely to affect men and women differently." The secretariat urged formulation of "gender inclusive policy measures to address climate change" and stressed that women "are important actors" and "agents of change" in coping and adaptation. The secretariat also named a gender coordinator and a group of "gender focal points" assigned to assure gender is brought into three of the UNFCCC programme areas.[15]

Gender refers to the differences in socially constructed roles and opportunities associated with being a man or a woman and the interactions and social relations between men and women. Gender is not only about women. Policies that aim to address any aspect of climate change will be less effective if they fail to take into account the differences between men, women, boys and girls. Gender-blind policies may exacerbate the problems associated with climate change by widening inequalities between the sexes.[16] Special attention may be required to compensate for inequalities that women currently face.

Given women's significant engagement in food production and preparation and the potential for land use to contribute to climate-change solutions in developing countries, the close connection between gender, farming and climate change deserves far more analysis than it currently receives. Because of greater poverty, lesser power over their own lives, less recognition of their economic productivity and their disproportionate burden in reproduction and child-raising, women face additional challenges as climate changes. The recent experiences of natural disasters—some logically related to climate change, others clearly not (See Box 4: What do tsunamis have to do with climate change?)—indicate that women are more likely to lose their lives and otherwise fare worse than men in extreme events from heat waves to hurricanes and tsunamis.

In Bonn in June 2009, a negotiating text drafted by the Ad Hoc Working Group on Long-Term Cooperative Action under the UNFCCC reflected the growing recognition of the importance of gender in the climate-change debate. The text included 13 references to gender, 17 references to women, and one reference to the Convention on the Eradication of All Forms of Discrimination Against Women. Greater participation of women in the climate issue—whether as scientists, community activists, or negotiators at conferences of the Intergovernmental Panel on Climate Change parties—can only benefit society's response to climate change by adding to the diversity of perspectives on how to address the challenge of climate change. This participation, in turn, can be aided by improving women's legal and social equality with men and their equal enjoyment of human rights, including the right to sexual and reproductive health and the determination of whether and when to bear children.

The Intergovernmental Panel on Climate Change, among the thousands of pages of its assessment reports, devoted one half page of text in 2007 to the issue of "gender aspects of vulnerability and adaptive capacity" in response to climate change and comparable natural disasters. Women,

 4 WHAT DO TSUNAMIS HAVE TO DO WITH CLIMATE CHANGE?

Because there is so little current or reliable research on many aspects of climate change, scientists must sometimes look at climate-change *proxies* for insights into how climate change affects women, men, boys and girls differently, or how each sex responds or adapts to natural disasters. Proxies are events that *resemble* climate change in some details.

Periodically, this report uses extreme events of many kinds as proxies. It considers the impacts of storms (which may be related to climate change), tsunamis (which clearly are not) and comparable natural disasters as one method of envisioning how climate change may affect migration, health, income-earning opportunities and gender relations in the coming years.

the box noted, "are disproportionately involved in natural resource-dependent activities, such as agriculture, compared to salaried occupations." Moreover, the "disproportionate amount of the burden endured by women during rehabilitation [from weather-related disasters] has been related to their roles in the reproductive sphere." The text concluded that the influence of gender in resilience to climate change impacts is "an important consideration" in developing interventions for adaptation, that gender differences related to adaptation "reflect wider patterns of structural gender inequality," and that a policy shift toward "more proactive capacity-building" was needed to reduce gender inequality.[17] Women, in fact, rarely make up more than about 15 per cent of the authors of the Panel's assessment reports.

Recent action

To arrive collectively at a set of agreements to accomplish the goals of climate change *mitigation* (reducing emissions or otherwise lowering atmospheric concentrations of greenhouse gases) and *adaptation* (minimizing social and economic disruption from climate change impacts), most of the world's nations have ratified the UNFCCC. The treaty, which entered into force in 1994, calls on the world's nations to "achieve stabilization of greenhouse-gas concentrations in the atmosphere at a level that would prevent dangerous anthropogenic interference with the climate system. Such a level should be achieved within a

POPULATION AND ADAPTATION

Thirty-seven of the 41 National Adaptation Programmes of Action, or NAPAs, that developing-country Governments had submitted to the UNFCCC by May 2009 explicitly link climate change and population and identify rapid population growth as a problem that either exacerbates the effects of climate change or hinders the ability of countries to adapt to it.[19] Through the preparation of NAPAs, the least developed countries state their priorities and needs for adapting to climate change. The growth of population can contribute to freshwater scarcity or degradation of cropland, which may in turn exacerbate the impacts of climate change. So too can population growth make it more difficult for Governments to alleviate poverty and achieve the Millennium Development Goals.

time-frame sufficient to allow ecosystems to adapt naturally to climate change, to ensure that food production is not threatened and to enable economic development to proceed in a sustainable manner."

The treaty recognizes the obligations countries have, not just to their own citizens but to future generations, and acknowledges the obligation of protecting the climate system "on the basis of equity and in accordance with their common but differentiated responsibilities and respective capabilities. Accordingly, the developed-country parties should take the lead in combating climate change and the adverse effects thereof."[18] It was to act on these principles that most nations ratified the 1997 Kyoto Protocol, designed to cap greenhouse-gas emissions by developed nations through 2012. The UNFCCC *encouraged* industrialized countries to stabilize greenhouse-gas emissions, while the Kyoto Protocol *committed them* to do so.

Agenda for positive change

Climate experts and Government officials from all over the world will converge in Copenhagen in December 2009 for the 15th Conference of Parties to the UNFCCC to hammer out a new international agreement that could lead to a cooler planet in the long run. Such an agreement would reduce emissions globally and equitably, build resilience to a changing climate, especially in those countries that have contributed the least to climate change but are most vulnerable to its impacts, and mobilize public

and political will to accomplish these tasks in ways that all nations can support in the long run. Negotiations will also address the need for financing and technology transfer to developing countries.

But what Governments must anticipate and prepare for today are the stresses climate change is likely to add to the already-challenging business of advancing development, alleviating poverty, assuring access to education and health care, and moving toward gender equality. Successful approaches to climate change are much more likely to emerge in the context of sustainable economic and social development, respect for human rights and cultural diversity, the empowerment of women and access to reproductive health for all.

Specific measures to address the problem must, however, be based on fact, not frenzy. Gaps in research on many of the effects of—and solutions to—climate change must be filled before it is too late.

The complex nature and momentum of human-induced climate change suggest three areas of action needed now, with immediate, near-term and long-term benefits.

Adaptation, now and for the duration: Some climate change has already taken place, and global temperatures are rising, so we have no choice but to adapt to the changes we face now and to anticipate those we can expect in the future. As temperatures are projected to rise for decades, and sea levels perhaps for centuries, learning to adapt and become more resilient to ongoing changes in climate is both an immediate and a long-term task. Adaptation, however, is not something that donor countries, banks or corporations can somehow bequeath to developing countries. Although financing and the transfer of technology and knowledge are essential to the effort, successful and lasting adaptation must arise from the lives, experience and wisdom of those who are themselves adapting. In the words of Byllye Avery, founder and former executive director of the National Black Women's Health Imperative in the United States, "When you are lifting a heavy basket, you must lift from the bottom."

Immediate mitigation: Without halting the rise in global emissions of greenhouse gases and then rapidly reducing them, adaptation to climate change will become an endless—and perhaps impossible—challenge. The push to build our resilience to climate change cannot distract from the need to reduce emissions as rapidly as possible, starting now.

Long-term mitigation: Critically needed early successes in reducing emissions will be a prelude to a task likely to preoccupy people for decades, even centuries: prospering globally while keeping human activities from sending the global atmosphere and climate outside the range of human habitability.

The 1994 International Conference on Population and Development, or ICPD, was a milestone in the history of population and development. At the conference, the world agreed that population is not about numbers, but about people. The conference's 20-year Programme of Action, adopted by 179 countries, argues that if needs for family planning and reproductive health care are met, along with other basic health and education services, then population stabilization will occur naturally, not as a matter of coercion or control.

There is good reason to believe that achievement of the ICPD's goal of universal access to reproductive health, in combination with improved education of girls and gender equality, would help achieve health and development objectives while also contributing to declines in fertility, which would in turn help reduce greenhouse-gas emissions in the long run. These fertility declines would by themselves—even in combination with increased maternal and child survival, to which reproductive health, education and gender equality also powerfully contribute— lead to population levels below those foreseen in most greenhouse-gas emission scenarios developed for the Intergovernmental Panel on Climate Change. A growing body of research indicates that stabilization of population will help reduce greenhouse-gas emissions in the long run. Universal access to voluntary family planning is one intervention that will help hasten this stabilization.

The representatives of Governments and non-governmental organizations who crafted the ICPD's Programme of Action achieved two remarkable advances that may offer lessons to those who are grappling with treaty and protocol language on climate change in Copenhagen in December 2009. One, they completed the transformation of population growth as a matter of human rights and the right of all people to make their own decisions regarding reproductive health. And two, they envisioned a means

6 "CLIMATE CHANGE," THE ICPD PROGRAMME OF ACTION AND THE MILLENNIUM DEVELOPMENT GOALS

The 1994 ICPD Programme of Action mentions "climate change" twice, first in its preamble as an ecological problem "largely driven by unsustainable patterns of production and consumption [and] adding to the threats to the well-being of future generations." The document calls for "increased international cooperation in regard to population in the context of sustainable development" but offers no specifics about how to marshal and apply this cooperation or the specifics of population's role in sustainable development. A second mention of climate change encourages Governments to "consider requests for migration from countries whose existence...is imminently threatened by global warming and climate change."[20]

Global concern about climate change grew in the years between the 1994 ICPD and the 2000 Millennium Development Goals. Ending the growth of greenhouse-gas emissions by 2015 is one of the targets for Millennium Development Goal 7, which aims at ensuring environmental sustainability. A 2008 report on the Goals mentions population growth in passing three times but does not explore population dynamics or their relationship with environmental sustainability or the other Goals.

by which personal self-fulfilment would contribute to the well-being of families, communities, nations and ultimately to the environmental sustainability of the world as a whole.

The Programme of Action is a model of what success could look like in the climate arena. In particular the world's nations may eventually conclude that a recognition of the right to development and to equal use of the global atmosphere and environment—coupled with the equal enjoyment of these and all rights by women, men, girls and boys, young and old—will cement an agreement by which all nations can abide.

The linkages between population and climate change are in most cases complex and indirect. But the nature of these linkages is becoming clear enough to arrive at the key recommendations of this report for mitigating climate change and aiding adaptation to it: elicit a new level of engagement by Governments in the areas of population and development, provide access to reproductive health and actively support gender equality.

1 Elements of climate change

The temperature of the earth's surface has risen 0.74 degrees Celsius in the past 100 years. This increase may not seem much, but this warming has been sufficient to disrupt many of the planet's ecosystems to pose significant risks to human well-being. More importantly, if recent trends continue or accelerate as many climate scientists predict, the earth's temperature may rise another four to six degrees by 2100, with likely catastrophic effect on the environment, habitats, economies and people.[1]

With growing confidence, climate scientists around the world attribute the bulk of recent warming to the greenhouse gases injected into the atmosphere as a result of the activities of an increasingly wealthy human population, particularly in the industrialized countries. Natural climate variation may explain some of the increase in temperatures since 1900. But scientists have so far found no natural causes—not changing solar conditions or an ongoing recovery from past ice ages—that can fully explain such a dramatic rise in temperatures. Nor can any natural forces explain why the 10 warmest years globally since 1880 have been in the last 13 years. (See Box 7)

Greenhouse gases, such as carbon dioxide and methane, occur naturally and create a "greenhouse effect"—so called because of an imperfect comparison to the glass walls of a greenhouse—that keeps the earth's surface warm. Without greenhouse gases, much more of the heat radiated from the sun would bounce back into space, and the earth's surface would be too cold to sustain life.

The additional greenhouse gases that come from intense burning of fossil fuels, modern farming methods that rely on fertilizers, and the industrial use of chlorofluorocarbons, particularly in the past 40 years, have thrown the earth's natural greenhouse effect into a state of disequilibrium. In addition, deforestation, clearing of other vegetation and the accumulation of carbon dioxide in the oceans have reduced the capacity of the world's "carbon sinks," which have for millennia absorbed excess carbon from the atmosphere. Less capacity to absorb carbon means there is more carbon dioxide in the atmosphere, exacerbating what now appears to be a runaway greenhouse effect.

As the earth's surface warms, weather patterns shift. Unreliable rains hamper food production. Melting ice in the Arctic is contributing to rising sea levels, endangering the lives of millions of people living in low-lying coastal areas around the world. Human-induced climate change threatens to cause shortages of fresh water for human

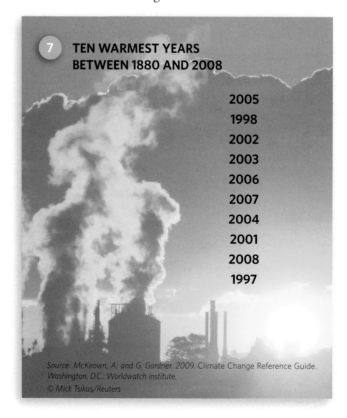

7 TEN WARMEST YEARS BETWEEN 1880 AND 2008

2005
1998
2002
2003
2006
2007
2004
2001
2008
1997

Source: McKeown, A.; and G. Gardner. 2009. Climate Change Reference Guide. Washington, D.C.: Worldwatch Institute.
© Mick Tsikas/Reuters

◀ *Lightning streaks across the night sky in Hefei, China. Storms will become more frequent and intense as the earth's atmosphere continues to warm.*
© Xinhua/Xinhua Press/Corbis

consumption and agriculture. More frequent and severe storms are likely, leading to devastating floods. And the warming atmosphere may be allowing diseases and pests once confined to tropical areas to spread north and south towards the poles.

There is alarming evidence that important "tipping points," leading to irreversible changes in climate or other earth systems, may already have been reached—or passed. Ecosystems as diverse as the Amazon rainforest and the Arctic tundra may be approaching thresholds of dramatic change through warming and drying. Mountain glaciers are in retreat, and the downstream effects of reduced water supply in the driest months will have repercussions that transcend generations.

In 2008, researchers using data from four different climate models found that changes in Arctic and Antarctic temperatures are not consistent with natural variability

Ecosystems as diverse as the Amazon rainforest and the Arctic tundra may be approaching thresholds of dramatic change through warming and drying. Mountain glaciers are in retreat, and the downstream effects of reduced water supply in the driest months will have repercussions that transcend generations.

and are directly attributable to human influence.[2] Evidence grew in 2008 that the Arctic sea ice is disappearing more rapidly than previously expected because of higher air and ocean temperatures.

For the second year in a row, there has been an ice-free channel in the Northwest Passage through the islands of northern Canada. This year also saw the opening of the Northern Sea Route along the Arctic Siberian coast. The two passages have probably not been open simultaneously in about 100,000 years, before the last ice age.

The overall declining trend of sea-ice in the Arctic has lasted at least three decades. The loss is greatest in summer, but is also evident in the reduced thickness of the winter ice packs. With less ice surviving the summer, the amount of thick ice that has built up over several years is decreasing. This leaves the whole sea-ice system more vulnerable to future warming and brings closer the prospect of an ice-free Arctic.[3]

8 GREENHOUSE GASES

The primary human-generated greenhouse gases are carbon dioxide, methane, fluorinated gases (including chlorofluorocarbons, infamous for their depletion of the upper atmosphere's protective ozone layer), and nitrous oxide. Greenhouse gases are the most important source of climate change. "Black carbon"—essentially soot and other small carbon particles from combustion—and changes in the reflectivity of the earth's surface (as when reflective sea ice melts and is replaced by heat absorbing ocean water) also contribute to warming.[4]

Greenhouse gas	Generated by
Carbon dioxide	Fossil-fuel combustion, land-clearing for agriculture, cement production
Methane	Livestock production, extraction of fossil fuels, rice cultivation, landfills, sewage
Nitrous oxide	Industrial processes, fertilizer use
Fluorinated gases	
• Hydrofluorocarbons	Leakage from refrigerators, aerosols, air conditioners
• Perfluorocarbons	Aluminum production, semiconductor industry
• Sulphur hexafluoride	Electrical insulation, magnesium smelting

In the Arctic the atmosphere is warming twice as fast as in most other parts of the world. In the far north, warming is amplified by a decrease in the reflectivity of the Earth's surface as ice and snow melt. Ice and snow reflect solar energy back into space, while darker surfaces like bare tundra and open ocean absorb more solar energy and then radiate it to heat the air above. So as the reflective surfaces disappear, the darker surfaces release heat into the immediate environment that results in more melt.

However, there may be other factors contributing to accelerated warming in the Arctic Ocean. In 2007, there was an especially large loss of ice in the Beaufort Sea, north of Canada and Alaska. This was due to incursions of warm water from the south that melted the ice from beneath.[5] Also, local atmospheric conditions amplified ice loss. Unnaturally clear, sunny skies in 2007, for example, increased melting in the 24-hour sun part of the year, and strong winds during the early part of the summer drove ice into seasonal packs, creating enlarged patches of open ocean.[6]

The largest mass of ice in the Arctic covers the island of Greenland. In places, the ice sheet is three kilometres thick. If all of it melts, it will raise sea levels by an esti-mated six metres. Until recently, glaciologists presumed that the ice would thaw slowly over millennia, as warming at the surface of the ice sheet permeates downward and gradually melts the ice. But the ice sheet is losing mass much faster than would be expected if normal melting alone was to blame. Current losses are more than 100 cubic kilometres a year. New findings in 2008 revealed that the flow into the ocean of the Jakobshavn Isbrae glacier in western Greenland, one of the most important routes for ice loss, has doubled since 1997.[7] A recent analysis of historical data on the extent of the Greenland ice sheet shows that total meltdown is quite possible as a result of warming on the scale that is being forecast for the next few decades.[8]

Antarctica is losing ice, too, particularly from the West Antarctic ice sheet. This sheet contains enough ice to raise sea levels by about five metres. Researchers estimated in 2008 that loss of ice from the West Antarctic ice sheet increased by 60 per cent from 1996 to 2006.[9] Ice loss from the Antarctic Peninsula, which extends from West Antarctica toward South America, increased by 140 per cent.

The most recent assessment by the Intergovernmental Panel on Climate Change forecast that global sea levels

⑨ CLIMATE TIPPING ELEMENTS

Scientists believe that several tipping elements could destabilize the planet's climate by setting off chain reactions—positive feedbacks—that accelerate other climate changes. Once a tipping element is triggered by crossing a threshold or tipping point, there is no turning back, even if all greenhouse-gas emissions were to end. Some tipping elements, such as the loss of Arctic summer sea ice, may be triggered within the next decade if climate change continues at the same rate. Others, such as the collapse of the Atlantic Ocean current, are thought to be many decades away, while the loss of Antarctic ice is unlikely to be complete for several centuries.[4]

Tipping element	Expected consequences
Loss of Arctic summer sea ice	Higher average global temperatures and changes to ecosystems
Melting of Greenland ice sheet	Global sea level rise up to six metres
Collapse of West Antarctic ice sheet	Global sea level rise up to five metres
Increase in El Niño events	Changes to weather patterns, including increased droughts, especially in Southeast Asia
Destruction of Amazon forests	Massive extinctions and decreased rainfall
Changes to India's summer monsoon	Widespread drought and changes in weather patterns
Changes to the Sahara/Sahel and the West African monsoon	Changes to weather patterns, including potential greening of the Sahara/Sahel—one of the few positive tipping elements

▲ *The lake is all that remains of a glacier near the rural town of Botijlaca, Bolivia. Bolivia's glaciers are melting rapidly, jeopardizing water supplies to rural and urban communities.*

© Andi Gitow/UNTV

would rise by between 18 and 59 centimetres in the coming century—just from the thermal expansion of warmer oceans and the melting of mountain glaciers. But since the report was completed, many researchers involved in that assessment have predicted that a much larger rise is possible or probable. The new prediction—of a one-metre rise by 2100—originates in part from reassessments of the potential for physical breakup of the ice sheets of Greenland and Antarctica.[10]

A 2008 study on the dynamics of ice-sheet loss argued that sea levels could rise by as much as two metres in the coming century as a result of outflows of ice from Greenland, Antarctica and other glaciers and ice caps.[11] Such a rise would be far beyond anything seen in the recent past. Sea levels rose 2 centimetres in the 18th century, 6 centimetres in the 19th century, and

19 centimetres in the 20th century; a rise equivalent to 30 centimetres is projected for the 21st century based on rates observed in the century's first few years.[12] The magnitude of scale for sea-level rise now being forecast would be in line with what happened at the end of the last ice age. Then, as ice sheets disintegrated, sea levels rose by between 70 and 130 centimetres per century.[13] Given current population densities of the areas affected, a one-metre rise in sea levels worldwide would displace around 100 million people in Asia, mostly eastern China, Bangladesh, and Vietnam; 14 million in Europe; and 8 million each in Africa and South America.[14]

Research in 2008 indicates that sea-level rise—from thermal expansion, mountain glacier retreat, and ice sheet melt—is likely to be much greater and to arrive much sooner than believed even two years ago. No matter how quickly climate change is mitigated, sea levels will rise. So, efforts to adapt to rising seas are more urgent than ever.

The Arctic contains very large stores of greenhouse gases in the form of methane locked in ice lattices in permafrost or beneath the bed of the Arctic Ocean, methane that may be released as the planet warms. Large-scale methane releases would exacerbate global warming and could turn natural ecosystems from carbon sinks to carbon sources, triggering a rapid and uncontrollable temperature increase.

Climate scientists are concerned that methane hydrates could escape into the atmosphere either as permafrost melts or as warmer waters destabilize frozen offshore deposits. In 2008, a study of the Siberian Shelf reported elevated methane concentrations offshore from the Lena River Delta.[15] Meanwhile, researchers showed that, once under way, thawing of east Siberian permafrost—thought to contain 500 billion tons of carbon—would be irreversible; 250 billion tons could be released in a century.[16] Northern peatland soils that are not frozen also contain large amounts of carbon and are vulnerable to warming. The peat's ability to store carbon is highly dependent on its moisture content. Warming will dry out the peat, lowering water tables. A new modelling study showed that this would lead to massive loss of organic carbon in the soil. In northern Manitoba, Canada, a 4-degree Celsius warming would release 86 per cent of the carbon that is sequestered, or stored away, in deep peat.[17]

One reason for fears about the ability of forests to soak up carbon dioxide is that forest cover itself is declining and is now contributing to emissions—1.5 billion tons of carbon a year enter the atmosphere from changes in land use, almost entirely from deforestation in the tropics.[18] Another reason is that even intact forests may be in trouble; the ability of forests to store carbon may have peaked, and rising temperatures may already be

Evidence is mounting for significant consequences to climate variability from soot, or black carbon that originates from fires, coal plants, diesel engines and burning by households. Dark particles that remain suspended in the atmosphere absorb radiant energy and warm the air they occupy. Global emissions of black carbon are rising fast.

decreasing carbon uptake by vegetation in the northern hemisphere. Higher temperatures impose significant stress on trees during the summer season, and photosynthesis halts sooner. Once photosynthesis halts, carbon is no longer sequestered, and stressed forests are vulnerable to damage from pollution, fires, pests and disease that can turn them into carbon sources.[19]

The other carbon sink—the oceans—is also in jeopardy. Oceans absorb carbon, helping maintain equilibrium in the earth's atmosphere. Over the past 150 years, the oceans have absorbed between one-third and one-half of the atmosphere's added carbon dioxide. As the absorbed gas combines with carbonate ions in seawater and forms carbonic acid, the oceans have become 30 per cent more acidic. The acidification inhibits marine life's ability to calcify, threatening shellfish and coral, which are an important source of food and incomes for many of the world's people.

There are other important human-induced influences on climate besides greenhouse gases. Evidence is mounting for significant consequences to climate variability from soot, or black carbon, that originates from fires, coal plants, diesel engines and burning by households. Dark particles that remain suspended in the atmosphere absorb radiant energy and warm the air they occupy. Global emissions of black carbon are rising fast, and Chinese emissions may have doubled since 2000. The warming influence of black carbon could be three times greater than estimates from the Intergovernmental Panel on Climate Change's latest report, making it the second-most important climatic agent after carbon dioxide.[20] These findings remain controversial because black soot can cool as well as warm. But when black carbon falls onto ice it darkens the surface, absorbing more of the sun's energy which leads to local warming and melting. Soot may be a contributor to the disappearance of glaciers in some regions and could even explain the accelerated rates of melt in the Himalaya-Hindu Kush.[21]

The average global temperature could rise by as much as 6.4 degrees Celsius by the end of this century.[24]

As much as 30 per cent of plant and animal species could become extinct if the global temperature increase exceeds 2.5 degrees Celsius.

One-third of the reef-building corals around the world could become extinct because of warming and acidifying waters.

Global average sea levels could rise by as much as 43 centimetres by the end of this century.

Arctic ice could disappear altogether during the summer by the second half of this century.

One in six countries could face food shortages each year because of severe droughts.

By 2075, between 3 billion and 7 billion people could face chronic water shortages.

New research demonstrates that winds in the strongest cyclones have become more intense in all oceans.[22] The increase has been greatest in relatively cool ocean basins that have seen the largest increases in sea temperatures, notably the North Atlantic, but also the eastern North Pacific and southern Indian oceans. Tropical cyclones form only when ocean temperatures exceed about 26 degrees Celsius. Therefore it is possible that warmer oceans may generate more frequent and more intense tropical cyclones.

Growing concern about world water shortages highlight new findings on the possible impacts that climate change will have on the earth's hydrologic cycle, including rainfall, soil evaporation, and loss of glacial meltwater flows in rivers. New findings predict empty reservoirs in the Mediterranean and American Midwest, dry rivers in China and the Middle East, and less predictable river flows characterized by flash floods in a glacier-free South Asia.[23]

The Intergovernmental Panel on Climate Change laid out a range of possible increases in global temperatures and possible impacts on society and the environment, ranging from modest and manageable to ones that can only be described as catastrophic. Unless action is taken

Figure 1.1: Extreme weather events, 1970-2005

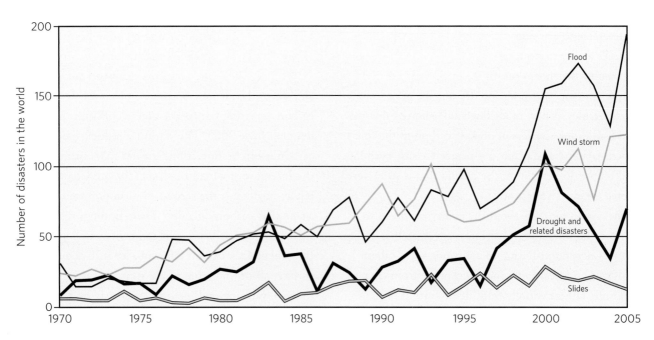

Source: United Nations International Strategy for Disaster Reduction. 2009.

soon to stabilize and then decrease concentrations of greenhouse gases in the atmosphere, there is a great risk that temperature increases could cause widespread damage to ecosystems, natural resources, human populations and disrupt economic activities. Such damage could certainly end prosperity in developed countries and threaten basic human livelihoods in developing countries.

Uncertainties remain in climate-change science. Still, the evidence available so far suggests that we may be within a few years of crossing tipping points, with potential to permanently disrupt seasonal weather patterns that have supported agricultural activities of half the human population, sustained carbon sinks, and prevented major ice sheets from melting.

11 BELIZEAN LIVELIHOODS THREATENED BY WARMING WATERS

Anita Cano, a 20-year-old woman with a quick smile, works the front desk at the Ambergris Diving Company in San Pedro, Belize. But she says she may not stay there for long. "It's not stable, because of the economy," she says.

Under normal circumstances, San Pedro is one of Belize's more vibrant tourism spots, bustling with foreigners in search of diving and snorkeling adventures on the nearby reef.

Tourism has taken a nosedive this year—most people say because of the global economic crisis. But there is also concern that dying coral reefs will make tourist destinations like Belize less attractive for the masses of visitors that each year help inject cash into the Belizean economy.

The tourism industry in Belize employs 15,000 people—about one in four jobs. Tourism is the country's largest employer of women, many of them single heads of households.

Scientists say that the corals off the coast of Belize and neighbouring countries are gradually dying due to effects of the climate change, such as higher water temperatures, stronger and more frequent hurricanes, as well as acidifica-

tion of the ocean as it absorbs more and more carbon dioxide from the air.

If there is a dramatic reduction of live corals along the Caribbean coast, tourism will not be the only sector to suffer. The country's 2,200 fishermen could find their livelihoods in peril. The fishing industry generates between 6 per cent and 8 per cent of Belize's gross domestic product. In addition, the likelihood of catastrophic consequences of stronger and more frequent hurricanes

Anita Cano.
© Trygve Olfarnes/UNFPA

would increase as the protection the coral reefs provide would literally erode.

Anita says she doesn't know much about the dying coral reef and other possible effects of climate change, but "90 per cent of people here depend on the ocean for their living, so of course it's important," she acknowledges.

"Business is down this year by 60 per cent compared to three to five years ago," says Andre Paz, a tour guide at Amigos del Mar Dive Shop in San Pedro, Belize. He, too, attributes the current decline in business to the global financial crisis, but also to the dying reef. "We see less fish, less coral and fewer colors out there," he says. Andre and his colleague Robert Zelaya believe climate change is the culprit.

Scientists say that corals are dying due to higher water temperatures, acidification of the ocean—a result of increased carbon-dioxide being absorbed into the water—and stronger and more frequent hurricanes.

As a result of the decline in business, Amigos del Mar has laid off four people and sold one of its 10 boats. "On an average day, we used to get 30 people going out diving, fishing or snorkeling. Now we get about 15," Paz says.

2 At the brink

The first order of business in dealing with human-induced climate change is to stop making it worse.

Actions now to reduce greenhouse-gas emissions in the future will help humanity avert disaster in the long run.

There is no time for delay; we are already at the precipice. The Intergovernmental Panel on Climate Change concluded in 2007 that even current concentrations of greenhouse gases could send temperatures past a 2-degree cumulative increase above the earth's average temperature before the Industrial Revolution began.[1] Based on assessments by the Panel and others of the probable impacts of various increases in global temperatures, many Governments and non-governmental organizations have accepted this 2-degree mark as the upper limit that should be respected to avoid potentially catastrophic human-caused climate change.[2]

The large volume of greenhouse gases already put into the atmosphere by human activity since the Industrial Revolution—but especially in the past 40 years—has given climate change so much momentum that only a concerted, comprehensive push by all nations and people stands a chance of slowing down or reversing the warming of the earth's surface.

All nations and all human beings have contributed in varying amounts to the atmosphere's heat-trapping burden, not just through emissions of carbon-dioxide from burning fossil fuels, but also through carbon dioxide related to land-use changes, from methane (more than half of it rising from farm fields), from nitrous oxide (more than four-fifths of these emissions are from agriculture), and from every other gas whose molecules hold more than two atoms together.[3]

From 1850 to 2002, countries we now call developed accounted for an estimated 76 per cent of cumulative carbon-dioxide emissions from fossil-fuel combustion, while the countries we now call developing accounted for an estimated 24 per cent, according to the World Resources Institute. The Institute's analysis of cumulative emissions, however, does not take into account emissions related to land-use changes or recent deforestation, much of which occurred in developing countries. Boosted by growing populations and rising affluence, the sum total of all developing countries' emissions began exceeding the totals of all those of developed countries in 2005 and now make up 54 per cent of the total, according to the Intergovernmental Panel on Climate Change. In 2007, China is believed to have overtaken the United States in total carbon-dioxide emissions resulting from fossil-fuel combustion.[4]

While developed countries contributed the majority of the increment in fossil-fuel carbon dioxide that has accumulated in the atmosphere since the Industrial Revolution began, the International Energy Agency projects that developing countries will account for the majority of the *growth* in total volume of carbon-dioxide emissions related to fossil fuels from 2008 through 2030.[5] With some exceptions, per capita emissions remain generally higher—and in many cases significantly higher—in developed than in developing countries.[6]

Although its role is difficult to quantify amidst the many factors contributing to emissions growth, population growth is among the factors influencing total emissions in industrialized as well as developing countries. Each additional person in a population will consume food and require housing, and ideally most will take advantage of transportation, which consumes energy, and may use fuel to heat homes and have access to electricity. The influence of additional population on increasing emissions is logically greatest where average per capita energy and material consumption levels are highest—that is, in developed countries. And although correlation does not prove causation, the International Energy Agency projects emissions to be lower in 2030 than today only in Europe and Japan, where population is now approaching or already in decline.[7]

The harsh realities of high per capita emissions among industrialized countries and swiftly rising ones among developing countries highlight the urgency of mobilizing all of humanity to stop collectively at the brink of this possible climate disaster zone. Climate scientists such as James Hansen of NASA, the United States National Atmospheric and Space Administration, and researchers at the Potsdam Institute for Climate Impact Research have suggested that the world should aim to stabilize carbon-dioxide concentrations *below* current levels of more than 380 parts per million. In effect, these scientists are saying, we should retreat from the brink by returning the atmosphere to the same state it was in around 1990.[8] A critical question for climate negotiators, Governments and the people of all countries is how responsibility for achieving such a retreat will be equitably allocated in a world in

which some populations have contributed disproportionately more to climate change.

Population change and emissions

The climate-science community generally points to the changing size and the pace and structure of population growth as integral to understanding climate change. This view is reflected in the Intergovernmental Panel on Climate Change's 2007 *Fourth Assessment Report*, which states that "gross domestic product per capita and population growth were the main drivers of the increase in global emissions during the last three decades of the 20th century."[9]

Research published by the International Energy Agency in 2006 tracked four major factors contributing to greenhouse-gas emissions from 1970 through 2000 and projected how these same four factors might lead to more or fewer emissions between 2000 and 2030. The research showed that rising per capita incomes have been and will be responsible for the largest share of emissions. Improvements in "energy intensity"—the amount of energy needed to generate a given amount of economic product—is accounting for a larger reduction in greenhouse-gas emissions over time. Meanwhile, population growth has been a smaller but consistent contributor to growth in energy-related carbon-dioxide emissions.[10]

Climate negotiators are beginning to raise population issues as part of the process leading to a new climate agreement in Copenhagen in December 2009. No Government or United Nations entity is suggesting to "control" population. Indeed, fear of appearing supportive of population control has until recently held back any mention of "population" in the climate debate. Nonetheless, some participants in the debate are tentatively suggesting the need at least to consider the impacts of population growth. The European Union has tabled a proposal that population trends be among the factors that should be taken into consideration when setting greenhouse-gas mitigation targets. The other factors are gross domestic product per capita, the "greenhouse-gas intensity" of countries' gross domestic product and past emission trends.[11]

Greenhouse-gas intensity reflects how a specific amount of greenhouse gases, measured in a uniform

Figure 2.1: Top 15 sources of cumulative carbon-dioxide emissions from fossil fuels, 1850-2002

Country	% of emissions worldwide
United States	29.3
EU-25	26.5
Russia	8.1
China	7.6
Germany	7.3
United Kingdom	6.3
Japan	4.1
France	2.9
India	2.2
Ukraine	2.2
Canada	2.1
Poland	2.1
Italy	1.6
South Africa	1.2
Australia	1.1

Source: *Baumert, K., T. Herzog and J. Pershing. 2005.* Navigating the Numbers: Greenhouse Gas Data and International Climate Policy. *World Resources Institute.*

way based on each gas' warming potential relative to carbon dioxide, is emitted with each currency unit (such as a dollar or euro) of economic activity. So if global greenhouse-gas intensity declines fast enough, the global economy can grow even while emissions shrink—the principal objective of climate policy, since most decision makers want economic growth but also want to reduce greenhouse-gas emissions. Some argue that patterns and levels of consumption are a more important influence on climate change than population growth. In the early 1990s, when a debate on this question was especially active among some researchers in both industrialized and developing countries, environment and development specialist Atiq Rahman of Bangladesh noted what he called the "extreme disparity" in per capita emissions and labelled *consumption*, rather than population, the "climate bomb." "Climate change is far more sensitive to consumption patterns than to demographic considerations," Rahman wrote, since "demographic dynamics are subject to greater inertial forces than consumption and production patterns.... [T]ackling consumption not only has sounder ethical foundations, but it also has greater scope for rapid action."[12]

The defense of consumption as the main arena for action on emissions reduction has faded little in the last two decades, perhaps in part because it shifts most of the blame for climate change to wealthier countries with patterns of higher consumption. "[T]he world's richest half-billion people—that's about 7 per cent of the global population—are responsible for 50 per cent of the world's carbon dioxide emissions," wrote environmental journalist Fred Pearce in 2009. "Meanwhile, the poorest 50 per cent are responsible for just 7 per cent of emissions."[13]

Still, calculations of the contribution of population growth to emissions growth globally produce a consistent finding that most of past population growth has been responsible for between 40 per cent and 60 per cent of emissions growth. Indian researchers Jyoti Parikh and J. P. Painuly noted during the early 1990s debate mentioned above that falling birthrates in the 1990s "could mean significant reductions in greenhouse-gas emissions [over what would otherwise occur] by 2100." Each birth results not only in the emissions attributable to that person in his or her lifetime, but also the emissions of all his or her descendents. Hence, the emissions savings from intended or planned births

Figure 2.2: Per capita greenhouse-gas emissions and cumulative population of regions

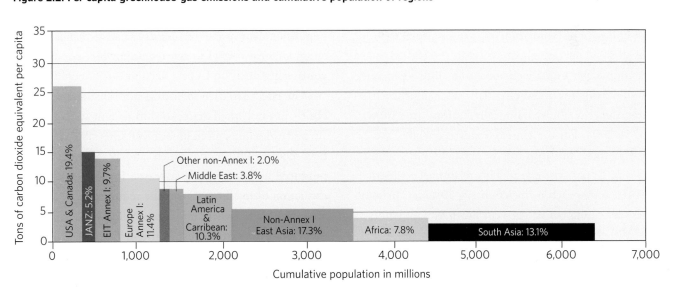

"Annex I" countries are those that UNFCCC considers developed. "Non-Annex I" countries are those that are developing. The chart reflects all cases for which data are available to the Intergovernmental Panel on Climate Change and reflects each group's equivalent global-warming potential in carbon dioxide. The percentages indicated for each country group refer to the proportion of global energy-related carbon-dioxide emissions. The figure shows that the average person in South Asia emits about three tons of carbon dioxide per year, while the average person in the United States and Canada emits more than 25 tons of carbon dioxide annually. JANZ: Japan, Australia, New Zealand. EIT: economies in transition.

Source: *Rogner, H.-H. and others. 2007. "Introduction." Climate Change 2007: Mitigation. Contribution of Working Group III to the Fourth Assessment Report of the Intergovernmental Panel on Climate Change. Cambridge: Cambridge University Press.*

POPULATION GROWTH SCENARIOS

The Population Division of the United Nations Department of Economic and Social Affairs has projected various scenarios for world population size in 2050, based on a variety of assumptions about fertility rates and other factors that influence growth. In the "low-variant" scenario, for example, nearly 8 billion people will inhabit the earth by 2050. This scenario assumes a fertility rate of 1.54, well under the 2.1 "replacement fertility" rate. Total fertility worldwide today is 2.56.

In its medium-variant scenario, the Population Division projects fertility in the less-developed regions as a whole to drop from 2.73 children per woman in 2005-2010 to 2.05 in 2045-2050. To achieve such reductions, the Population Division states, it is essential that access to voluntary family planning expands, particularly in the least developed countries. Around 2005, the use of modern contraceptive methods in the least developed countries was 24 per cent among women of reproduc-

tive age who were married or in a union. Another 23 per cent of such women were not using contraception, despite a wish not to become pregnant now or within the next two years—the definition of "unmet need."[18] According to the United Nations Secretary-General, in a report on world population and the ICPD Programme of Action, there are an estimated 106 million married women in developing countries who have an unmet need for family planning.[19]

World population scenarios, 2050		
Low	**Medium**	**High**
7.959 billion	9.150 billion	10.461 billion
World fertility rates, 2045 to 2050, by population growth scenario		
Low	**Medium**	**High**
1.54	2.02	2.51

multiply with time. One reason for this assessment of population growth and greenhouse-gas emissions is the large influence of population increases on total emissions in some developed countries. In the United States, for example, per capita emissions of fossil fuel-generated carbon dioxide remained essentially unchanged even during the generally economically healthy years from 1990 to 2004. For the United States as a whole, the country's total emissions rose in parallel with its population, at 18 per cent a year. This relationship varied, however, across each of the country's 50 states. In some states, per capita emissions went down as populations rose, and vice versa.

In 1991, physicist John P. Holdren, now chief science advisor to U.S. President Barack Obama, noted that "changes in settlement patterns necessitated by population growth result in more transport, per person, of resources, goods, and people," making a case that population growth directly stimulates consumption growth. Other increases in energy consumption, he suggested,

might result in more use of air conditioning if densely populated urban areas create "heat islands" or "if population density and distribution create demands for energy-intensive services not required when population was smaller."[14]

The effect Holdren identified now challenges some efforts in the United States to shift to renewable energy. By one estimate, a given amount of renewable energy may require 300 times as much land as the same energy produced by fossil fuels. The reason for this is that the extraction of fossil fuels generally requires only a limited amount of land, where mines or drilling wells transfer them from the earth's crust to the surface. Solar power, by contrast, is based on large areas of photovoltaic cells or mirrors capturing and concentrating the power of sunlight over large land areas. Wind power generally requires large fields on which many giant turbines may be placed. Environmentalists and U.S. Government officials alike worry the land hunger of renewable energy projects will add to already stiff competition between

▲ Zimbabwean farmer Mabel Zevezanayi holds a dried corn cob in Bikita District, affected by drought.
© AFP/Getty Images

human and ecosystem needs, especially in the western United States.[15]

The approach to population dynamics endorsed in the Programme of Action of the International Conference on Population and Development (ICPD) for developing countries—respecting reproductive rights and providing universal access to sexual and reproductive health services, including voluntary family planning—is appropriate to developed countries as well. Rates of unintended pregnancies are actually higher in the industrialized countries than in the developing ones, according to the Guttmacher Institute, which studies the phenomenon in both blocs. In Europe, Australia, Canada, Japan, New Zealand and the United States, an average of 41 per cent of all pregnancies are unintended.[16] In the developing countries, an estimated 35 per cent of pregnancies are unintended. Preventing unintended pregnancies could contribute to population stabilization in the long run and may in turn contribute to a reduction in greenhouse-gas emissions in the future.[17]

Population and climate change: a closer look

A report of the Secretary-General to the United Nations Commission on Population and Development's 42nd session in early 2009 takes a more nuanced view of the relationship between population, development, greenhouse-gas emissions and climate change. The report, prepared by the Population Division, linked the rapid growth of world population in the 20th century with even more rapid growth of urban population, production, land in cultivation, water use and energy consumption. "Together," the report suggested, these trends "are having unprecedented impacts on the environment, causing climate change, land degradation and loss of biodiversity."

The influence of population growth on emissions, however, is complicated by the other forces. According to the Population Division, "The relation between population growth and increasing greenhouse-gas emissions is not straightforward, and the scenarios of future emission trends do not permit assessing the effects of population dynamics net of economic and technological changes. Furthermore, changing population age structures, increasing urbanization and changes in household size interact in affecting emissions."[20]

Researchers began dissecting the impacts of population change on emissions only in the mid-1990s. Among the early findings was one in 1995 that reductions in household size, which often accompany lower fertility and higher economic growth, could significantly increase total greenhouse-gas emissions. These researchers found that homes are basic units of energy consumption and tend to be heated or cooled whether occupied by a family of seven or by a single person. Indeed, so strongly did the reduction in household size appear to boost emissions that demographers in the International Institute of Applied Systems Analysis' World Population Program stated, "A divorce may cause more carbon dioxide emissions than an additional birth."[21]

The importance of smaller households in elevating emissions, affirmed by a 2004 study quantifying such impacts, underlines the fact that population growth occurs in specific contexts that can enhance or dampen its influence on the environment.[22] Even the demographic unit—an individual or household, for example—might significantly alter the outcome of emissions models. The effect of smaller households on emissions led some

13 WOMEN, MEN AND GREENHOUSE-GAS EMISSIONS

If greenhouse-gas emissions begin with individual human activities, might those of women somehow be different from those of men? There is little research that aims to answer this question, particularly in developing countries. And in the developed countries, there have been only a handful of public opinion surveys on climate change or other environmental issues that disaggregate results by sex.

According to research published by the Organization for Economic Cooperation and Development in 2008, women in industrialized countries are more likely to be "sustainable consumers," meaning, for example, that they tend to buy ecologically friendly and organic foods, are more likely to recycle and are more interested in efficient energy use. Women in these countries account for as much as 80 per cent of consumer decisions, the research shows.[26]

It is unclear, however, whether consumption patterns that contribute less to the warming of the atmosphere are the result of women's environmentally conscious decisions at the household level or the result of chronic economic and social inequalities that prevent women from benefiting from and contributing to their countries' and communities' development. Several gender-specific studies of attitudes about the environment or climate change in the United States generally support the view that women are more likely than men to buy "green" products, which are advertised as less detrimental to the environment. Women were also generally less likely than men to trust Governments and corporations to solve environmental problems and somewhat more likely to want to take action personally on them. These gender-based differences were more pronounced at higher incomes.[27] In one study conducted in 22 countries, researchers found women were somewhat more likely to care about environmental problems such as climate change and to change their behaviour as a result.[28]

In Sydney, Australia, a 2008 survey of suburban residents about environmental sustainability found women and girls easier to attract to cooperative initiatives, more socially focused, and more concerned about the impacts of climate change. Men and boys were less likely to get involved in sustainability and more drawn to technology, governance issues and business in discussing environmental issues.[29]

Nordic researchers have probed the implications of differences in emissions and found women in developed—and developing—countries to have less impact on the atmosphere overall. The chief reason seems to be that the two sexes move differently from place to place, with men more likely than women to drive a car (75 per cent more likely in Sweden[30]) and to fly in airplanes. This difference, however, appears to stem more from unequal access to economic resources and less influence over decision-making than from behaviour or attitudes regarding the environment or transportation generally. The study also quantified another differential in greenhouse-gas-related consumption: men in developed countries eat more meat—139 grams daily in Denmark on average, compared to 81 grams for Danish women. Not only do women eat less in proportion to their body size, but at least in some countries they consume a more vegetable-oriented and less meat-based diet.

researchers to speculate that population *ageing*, the increase in the average age of a population as life expectancy increases and fertility declines, might lead to *rising* emissions—at least partially offsetting emissions savings resulting from the slowdown in growth itself. Studies of ageing itself have, however, produced conflicting findings. A group of researchers associated with United States and European research institutions found ageing to *reduce* emissions significantly in the United States and somewhat less significantly in India and China.[23] Although older people are likely to live in smaller households than younger people, the researchers found, the impact will be more than offset by the slower economic growth and reduced consumption presumed to accompany an ageing population.

Urbanization works in the opposite direction, some of these same researchers found. A shift of population from rural areas to cities appears likely to boost emissions substantially. This is not necessarily because people who live in cities contribute more on a per capita basis to greenhouse-gas emissions than those who live in rural areas. Other researchers, however, have argued that this is a myth and that urban areas now contribute much less than half the world's greenhouse-gas emissions despite being home to more than half the world's people.[24] The economic growth stimulated in cities tends to have a ripple effect throughout a country, helping boost economic growth in rural areas as well. In turn, greater economic growth may therefore boost greenhouse-gas emissions throughout a whole country.[25] In general, economic change continually reveals itself as the more *immediate* influence on greenhouse-gas emissions than population change.

Population and future emissions

No human is genuinely "carbon neutral," especially when all greenhouse gases are figured into the equation. Therefore, everyone is part of the problem, so everyone must be part of the solution in some way. The world's Governments and peoples will need to work together on every aspect of the factors that increase greenhouse-gas emissions. One such factor is the earth's growing population.

If the United Nations Population Division's low population growth scenario—about 8 billion people by the year 2050—materializes, it might result in 1 billion

A woman works in her cornfield near a coking factory in Changzhi, Shanxi Province, China.
© Reuters

to 2 billion fewer tons of carbon emissions than if the medium-growth scenario—a little more than 9 billion people by 2050—materializes, according to climate scientist Brian O'Neill of the National Center for Atmospheric Research.[31] Others have estimated comparable emissions savings by 2050 through the application of known energy-efficiency techniques in all new buildings worldwide or by erecting 2 million 1-gigawatt wind turbines to displace coal-fired power plants currently in use.[32] Moreover, the annual emissions savings would continue to grow substantially after the middle of the century as world population peaked and began declining, compared to continued population growth assumed in the medium-growth projection. This means that the net emissions savings achieved through a low population growth scenario would be equivalent to the net emissions savings achieved through major investments in energy technologies in a medium population growth scenario.

British economist Nicholas Stern estimated that in order to keep global temperatures from crossing into a potentially catastrophic zone, "global average per capita [greenhouse-gas] emissions...will—as a matter of basic arithmetic—need to be around two tons by 2050," assuming a world population of 9 billion people and speaking in terms of carbon dioxide equivalents. "This figure is so low that there is little scope for any large group to depart significantly above or below it."[33]

If the world followed the trajectory of the United Nations Population Division's low-variant projection of 8 billion people, the earth's atmosphere would be able to tolerate higher per-capita emissions, since fewer people would be emitting greenhouse gases.[34] The low-variant projection assumes lower fertility rates that might result from increased access to reproductive-health services, including

family planning, and other actions to increase opportunities and freedoms for women and girls. One study of the cost of averting a fixed amount of fossil-fuel carbon-dioxide emissions found that dollar-for-dollar, investments in voluntary family planning and girls' education would also in the long run reduce greenhouse-gas emissions at least as much as the same investments in nuclear or wind energy.[35]

According to a 1992 report by a committee of the United States National Academy of Sciences, "family planning impacts on greenhouse-gas emissions are important at all levels of development." The committee concluded, "The reduced population growth associated with higher income growth...offsets in large part the higher greenhouse-gas emissions associated with faster economic growth. The family planning effects indicate that, as of 2020, carbon emissions will be about 15 per cent lower for the lower-, middle- and upper-middle-income countries than they would be without family

WOMEN AND REFORESTATION

The relative dearth of research on gender aspects of deforestation is surprising, given the strong connection between fuelwood and activities such as cooking and the firing of ceramics. Research shows that in many developing countries, women must walk farther and farther to gather fuel. In one rural community in Sudan, for example, the time required quadrupled over a single decade. Moreover, the livelihoods of women in rural areas often depend on forest resources. Loss of forests may therefore undermine income-earning opportunities. Finally, loss of forests often affects women's health: carrying heavy loads of fuelwood over long distances can result in spinal damage, complicate pregnancies and increase the risk of maternal mortality.

In recent decades, however, such women-focused non-governmental organizations as the Green Belt Movement in Kenya and the Women's Environment and Development Organization in the United States have mobilized to protect and even expand forested lands. Many such groups also advocate for or help ensure compliance with environmental treaties.

Sociologists at three United States universities—the State University of New York at Stony Brook, Brown, and Clark—recently examined deforestation in 61 nations between 1990 and 2005 and found that countries with large or numerous women's and environmental non-governmental organizations showed significantly lower levels of forest loss. The researchers suggested that women's non-governmental organizations achieved what theory might predict: they advocated successfully for forest protection and mobilized activity that had a net positive effect on forest conservation.[40]

planning. Strong family planning programmes are in the interests of all countries for greenhouse-gas concerns as well as for broader welfare concerns."[36]

Investing in women and girls in ways that improve their health, well-being and status in their societies leads to reductions in fertility rates and will thus contribute to a reduction in greenhouse-gas emissions in the long run.

Women and emissions reduction

There may be opportunities to tailor efforts to reduce emissions and to pull carbon out of the atmosphere more effectively by considering gender differences in any discussion about consumption.

Women produce roughly half the world's food, according to the Food and Agriculture Organization of the United Nations, and anywhere from 60 per cent to 80 per cent of food in most developing countries.[37] Natural land-based carbon sequestration—the potential of farm and forest soils, trees, perennial crops and other plants to absorb carbon and keep it out of the atmosphere for decades—is attracting increasing interest as every possibility for holding down greenhouse-gas concentrations is pursued. If financial instruments could be devised to encourage such practices—as seems likely to occur as climate change impacts become more obvious

and damaging—women farmers could be at the forefront of mitigation efforts.[38] This could have a substantial impact on women's livelihoods as well, assuming laws are restructured and cultural norms shift as needed in some countries so that women can own the land they farm and control the income they earn.

Already, the world has witnessed the power of women to take actions that contribute to lower levels of atmospheric carbon dioxide. Wangari Maathai won the Nobel Peace Prize for a lifetime of environmental activism that began by mobilizing women to plant tens of thousands of trees in deforested and degraded soils of Kenya. In India, the Chipko movement drew women, the original "tree huggers," as early as the 1970s to protect forests and their own forestry rights by linking hands and arms around trees to dissuade the loggers assigned to fell them. The movement led to major reforms in Indian forestry laws that resulted in greater forest cover today (and hence more carbon in trees and less in the atmosphere) than would otherwise be the case. One study of deforestation, an activity performed overwhelmingly by men and responsible for a substantial proportion of all carbon-dioxide emissions, found that a high presence of women's non-governmental organizations in low-income countries may help protect forests against destruction.[39]

3 On the move

The environment has always shaped the movement of people and the distribution of the human population across the planet. Throughout history, people have left places with harsh or deteriorating conditions, and nomadic peoples have traditionally opted for seasonal migration to maintain their livelihoods in sensitive ecosystems. The droughts between 1930 and 1936 in the American "Dust Bowl" displaced hundreds of thousands of people, and the droughts that struck Africa's Sahelian region in the 1970s forced millions of farmers and nomads towards cities.[1]

But over the last two decades, the nature and scale of environmentally induced population movements have begun to change. While no reliable figures exist, the growing certainty about the impacts of climate change suggest that an increasing number of people will migrate mainly for environmental reasons in the future. Although the geography and scale of future movements of people is less easy to predict than the details of climate change itself, the probability is high that changes in sea levels, climate and other environmental conditions will spur major increases in movement in the coming decades. Societies would do well to consider now how to address environmentally influenced movements of people.

The relationship between environmental factors and human mobility is complex: on the one hand, environmental change triggers human movement. On the other hand, migration and displacement may take a toll on the environment—in areas of origin, areas of destination and the travel routes in between. Such a two-way connection between migration and the environment can result in a vicious circle: population movement contributes to environmental degradation in the area of destination, which may in turn provoke further migration and displacement. Environmental degradation refers to processes, such as rising sea levels, which can be caused or exacerbated by climate as well as by human activity through, for example, land degradation resulting from overly intensive farming.

In most cases, it is difficult to establish a simple and direct causal relation between the movement of people and environmental degradation. The links between the two are often complicated by other factors, such as conflict, governance and levels of development.

Climate change and human mobility

As early as 1990, the Intergovernmental Panel on Climate Change stated that "one of the gravest effects of climate change may be those on human migration."[2] This statement was substantiated by the Panel's 2007 *Fourth Assessment Report*, which showed that climate change is likely to raise the risk of humanitarian emergencies and trigger population movements as a result of increasingly intense weather events, sea-level rise and accelerated environmental degradation.[3]

Climate change and its adverse consequences for livelihoods, public health, food security, and water availability will have a major impact on human mobility, likely leading to a substantial rise in the scale of migration and displacement. Such environmentally induced movements are likely to take place mostly within countries but also to a lesser extent across national borders.[4] The effects of climate change may also render some people stateless.

The numbers gap

While many experts agree that climate change is expected to become one of the key factors prompting population movement in the next decades, there is still uncertainty about the scale and nature of the impacts of climate change and about the best policies and strategies for addressing the problem. One reason for the uncertainty is the dearth

◀ *An Indian villager carries her belongings through flood waters in the village of Sandeshkhali, 100 kilometres southeast of Kolkata.*
© AFP/Getty Images

of reliable data. But despite the shortage of hard data, it is evident that environmental changes are already resulting in substantial human migration and displacement.

Recorded natural disasters[5] have doubled from approximately 200 a year to over 400 a year over the past two decades, with seven out of every 10 disasters recorded as "climate-related."[6] The total number of people suffering the impacts of these natural disasters has tripled over the past decade, with an average of 211 million people directly affected each year.[7] The annual average "humanitarian toll" of climate-related disasters was an estimated 165 million people in the 30 years between 1973 and 2003, amounting to a staggering 98 per cent of all persons killed or affected by natural disasters within that period.[8] There are also indications that this figure is on the rise: from 1998 to 2007, 2.2 billion people were affected by climate disasters compared to 1.8 billion in the 10 previous years.[9]

There are various estimates for the number of people already displaced by environmental changes, with 25 million being the most widely quoted figure.[10] This figure does not include a potentially greater number of people who moved as a result of gradual environmental changes, such as drought or soil erosion. The figure also does not take into account those who have been displaced by other adverse consequences of climate change, such as diminished food security.

Estimating future climate change-related population flows presents an even greater challenge, with figures ranging wildly from 50 million to 1 billion people by the middle of the century, either within their countries or across borders, on a permanent or temporary basis.[11] The most widely used estimate of people to be displaced by environmental factors by 2050 is 200 million.[12]

Large discrepancies among the various estimates raises important questions not only about the reliability and

NO PLACE LEFT TO GO

These days, when Oreba Obiin takes a step out of her home, she steps into the sea. Oreba and her husband Titera live in an *auti*, or open hut, with their two sons, a few chickens, three piglets and a dog, part of the *Tebike Inano* community on low-lying coastal Tarawa, in their atoll nation of Kiribati.

Oreba, 51, has seen the sea change, especially in the past decade. The water is rising, she says, explaining that she and her husband have already had to add sand to their home's floor several times to keep it dry. "In the beginning our roof was very high. Now the roof is getting really close to us. If we keep adding sand to the floor, my head will soon touch the ceiling."

Many inhabitants of Tarawa have built sea walls along the shoreline to protect their land, but if the sea continues to rise, the sea walls won't suffice. "We want to stay here...but if we have to move, then we have no choice," Oreba says.

But where will Oreba and thousands like her go?

Kiribati consists of 33 atolls, tiny specks of narrow land made of coral, sand and limestone, barely three metres above sea level, in the middle of the vast Pacific Ocean. These islets are especially vulnerable to the impacts of global warming, ranging from rising seas, more violent storms, coastal erosion and the

Oreba Obiin, 51, combats coastal erosion in Kiribati by planting mangrove seedlings.
© Reethu Arjun/UNPFA

intrusion of salt into fresh-water tables. On some of the outer atolls, entire villages have already been washed away. Unlike other low-lying countries, however, the people of Kiribati have no higher ground to retreat to.

"Adaptation has very severe limitations for us," explains Kiribati's President Anote Tong. "If we move away from the shoreline we are already on the other shoreline, on the other side of the island."

Tong has set a clear course for dealing with short-term adaptation measures on the one hand and finding long-term solutions, on the other. "We will continue to live here for as long as we are able to live and will continue to need what we have needed over the years, so investments in infrastructure will have to carry on," Tong says. "But what options do we have if we don't relocate? We drown, don't we? We have to relocate. If we relocate to another country, of course we would lose some of the culture. But if we don't, we would lose the entire nation and our people. It's not a choice, it's a necessity."

availability of data, but also about the methodologies and definitions used to collect and analyse the information and about underlying assumptions made by the people looking at the numbers. Developing reliable estimates of climate change-related population flows is fraught with challenges, including the complex relationship between environmental factors and human mobility, uncertainty about climate-change impacts and scenarios, and the need to account for other variables, such as demographic trends and projections.[13] In addition, environmental processes and migration responses vary in time and space, further complicating the analysis.

The absence of generally agreed terminology is another challenge. The popular terms "climate refugee" or "environmental refugee" have no basis in existing international refugee law. Often those persons referred to as "climate refugees" have not actually crossed an international border. The use of such terminology can exacerbate confusion regarding the link between climate change, environmental degradation and migration.

Substantial environmentally induced population flows are likely in the future, and these flows will have implications for humanitarian relief and migration management. Even low-end estimates of slow or sudden population movements would pose enormous global challenges. Meeting the needs of additional millions leaving home as a result of climate change-related factors would severely test the efficacy and sustainability of humanitarian response models currently employed by the United Nations and international relief organizations.

Myths vs. reality

Suggestions that millions of environmental migrants are poised to flee developing countries to permanently seek safety and new lives in industrialized countries are misleading.

16 DEFINITIONS OF PEOPLE WHO ARE ON THE MOVE

There is no international consensus on terminology about people who move in response to climate-related factors. The International Organization for Migration has proposed a working definition of "environmental migrants" as "persons or groups of persons who, for compelling reasons of sudden or progressive changes in the environment that adversely affect their lives or living conditions, are obliged to leave their habitual homes, or choose to do so, either temporarily or permanently, and who move either within their country or abroad."[14]

Internally displaced persons
The currently accepted definition of internally displaced persons is "persons or groups of persons who have been forced or obliged to flee or to leave their homes or places of habitual residence, in particular as a result of or in order to avoid the effects of armed conflict, situations of generalized violence, violations of human rights or natural or human-made disasters, and who have not crossed an internationally recognized State border." This definition includes all those forcibly displaced within their country due to the effects of climate change.

Refugees
Under international law, a refugee is a person who "owing to well-founded fear of persecution for reasons of race, religion, nationality, membership of a particular social group or political opinions, is outside the country of his nationality and is unable or, owing to such fear, is unwilling to avail himself of the protection of that country, or who, not having a nationality and being outside of the country of his former habitual residence as a result of such events, is unable or, owing to such fear, is unwilling to return to it." The United Nations High Commissioner for Refugees has a mandate to protect, as refugees, persons who fear serious and indiscriminate threats to life, physical integrity or freedom resulting from generalized violence or events seriously disturbing public order, in addition to persons falling within the 1951 Refugee Convention (1951 Convention Relating to the Status of Refugees) definition. These definitions exclude anyone who crosses borders solely because of environmental degradation in their nations of origin.

Stateless persons
A stateless person is defined as "a person who is not considered as a national by any state under the operation of its law. Persons who possess a nationality in formal terms but whose nationality is ineffective are generally referred to as "de facto stateless persons." Additionally, a "stateless refugee" is defined in the 1951 Refugee Convention as a person "who, not having a nationality and being outside the country of his former habitual residence as a result of such events, is unable or, owing to such fear, is unwilling to return to it."

Overall, environmental migration is—and is likely to continue to be—mainly an internal phenomenon, with a smaller proportion of movement taking place between neighbouring countries, and even smaller numbers migrating long distances beyond the region of origin. Furthermore, a number of studies, such as one in rural Mali during the 1983 to 1985 drought, revealed that environmental degradation may actually contribute to a decline in the rates of international, long-distance moves.[15] This is likely due to the relatively high cost of long-distance migration, which fewer households can afford in drought years. When long-distance migration does take place, the destination is usually based on the location of existing support networks, established or traditional migration routes and, in many cases, the historical ties between the country of origin and the country of destination. Many environmentally induced population movements are temporary; many people prefer to return home as soon as it's safe and feasible.

The majority of environmental migrants have so far come from rural areas within the least developed countries. But in the future, there may indeed be unprecedented levels of environmentally induced migration out of urban areas, as rising seas threaten to inundate densely populated coastal areas, where 60 per cent of the world's 39 largest metropolises are located, including 12 cities with populations of more than 10 million.[16]

Environmental drivers

In some cases, extreme weather events, such as cyclones, drive people from their homes, but in many more cases, insidious environmental degradation provides the impetus for leaving. Not all environmental degradation is related to climate change, and therefore not all movements in response to environmental degradation are related to climate change.

It is likely that both extreme weather events and changes in mean temperatures, precipitation and sea levels will in many cases contribute to increasing levels of mobility. But there are inherent difficulties in predicting with any precision how climate change will impact on population distribution and movement. This is partly because of the relatively high levels of uncertainty about the specific effects of climate change, and partly because of the lack of comprehensive data on migration flows, especially movements within national boundaries and in particular for low-income countries that are likely to be most affected by climate change.[17]

 17 **CLIMATE-CHANGE SCENARIOS AND THEIR IMPACT ON POPULATION MOVEMENTS**

According to the Intergovernmental Panel on Climate Change's *Fourth Assessment Report,* population movements may be triggered by increases in the areas affected by droughts, increased tropical cyclone activity, increased incidence of extreme high sea-level rise (excluding tsunamis) and increased climate variability.[18] Meanwhile, Walter Kälin, Representative of the United Nations Secretary-General on the Human Rights of Internally Displaced Persons, has identified five climate change scenarios, each of which has a different impact on the pace or scale of migration or displacement:

- *Hydro-meteorological disasters,* including extreme weather events such as hurricanes, flooding and mudslides, which may lead to sudden-onset displacement.
- *Environmental degradation,* including desertification, water scarcity and soil exhaustion, which may result in gradual migration or displacement.
- *Losses in state territory,* including erosion and coastal flooding resulting from rising sea levels. Persons living in low-lying coastal areas and the so-called "sinking" small island developing states, such as the Maldives, Tuvalu and Vanuatu, will be most affected by this scenario. It may lead to gradual migration and displacement, and possibly even to statelessness.
- *Designation of "high risk" areas by national authorities,* including territories that are prone to disasters and that are designated as unsafe, leading to the forced relocation of its inhabitants. This scenario may cause gradual migration, relocation and displacement, most often within the same state.
- *Violence and armed conflict over scarce and diminishing natural resources,* including conflict arising from food and water insecurity and lack of arable land. This scenario may cause both gradual and sudden migration and displacement.

For a clearer picture of human mobility and environmental change, it is useful to distinguish between the effects of sudden events or natural disasters and slow-onset processes. Both influence population mobility patterns but in different ways.

Natural disasters, including those related to climate change, may destroy basic infrastructure, disrupt services and undermine livelihoods, often resulting in sudden, large-scale movements of people. For instance, Hurricane Katrina, which hit the United States in August 2005, displaced about 1 million people.

Many people who leave their homes in the wake of natural disasters eventually return. But the ability to leave disaster-stricken areas and return to them is influenced by factors such as perceived risk, socio-economic status and mitigation through aid and subsidies.

While major natural disasters, such as Cyclone Nargis in Myanmar, claim most of the world's headlines, the less-dramatic but equally devastating gradual environmental changes go largely unnoticed by the international media. Yet it is these gradual changes, including desertification, water scarcity and coastal and soil erosion, that are responsible for the majority of environmentally induced population movements.

In Africa, for instance, an estimated 10 million people are likely to have migrated or been displaced over the last two decades mainly in response to environmental degradation and desertification.[19]

Gradual environmental changes can produce a variety of migration flows, with the majority likely to occur internally or across borders into neighbouring countries.

Different stages of environmental degradation can be expected to have different outcomes for the movement of people. At early and intermediate stages of environmental degradation, migratory responses are often temporary in nature and are more likely to be non-forced. When environmental degradation becomes severe or irreversible, as in cases of sea-level rise, resulting displacement can become permanent and requires resettlement of affected populations.

Some areas may be exposed to a combination of gradual environmental degradation and natural disasters. In such cases, degradation can substantially increase the vulnerability of the area to the effects of natural disasters.

Compounding factors

The relationship between environmental factors and the movement of people can both affect and be affected by conflict. Changes in population distribution associated

---

 MANAGING CLIMATE-INDUCED POPULATION MOVEMENTS IN NEPAL

Repeated flooding in eastern and western Nepal in August 2008 affected more than 250,000 people, many of whom were living in poverty and had already endured floods and landslides a year earlier.

Floods and landslides are seasonal disasters in Nepal and are linked to the clearing of the forests, particularly in hilly areas. Climate change is expected to further exacerbate the frequency and intensity of flooding, as rains spread westward across the country and melting snow and glaciers cause already-swollen rivers to overflow their banks in the rainy season.

Nepal ranks among countries with a low "human development index," with over 80 per cent of the population surviving on less than $2 per day.

Gender is one of the factors influencing vulnerability to natural disasters in Nepal. As more and more males migrate from mountainous regions and rural areas to newly developed cities, more and more women are becoming heads of households, remaining in areas prone to flooding and are therefore most vulnerable to climate-related disasters.

In eastern Nepal in 2008, a retaining wall along the Koshi River collapsed, washing away whole villages in the Sunsari and Saptari districts and affecting about 70,000 people. The force of the water was so strong that the river's course changed almost completely, blocking access to some flooded areas and stranding tens of thousands of people in makeshift camps. In response to the catastrophe, the International Organization for Migration led the coordination of the international humanitarian response of the United Nations, the Red Cross and Red Crescent, non-governmental organizations and other actors to assist the Government of Nepal in addressing urgent humanitarian needs while laying the foundation for more durable solutions and building national capacities for disaster-risk reduction, paving the way for safe, voluntary and orderly returns.

▲ *Man runs for shelter from storm near Niamey, Niger.*
© AFP/Getty Images

with environmental degradation and climate change can lead to increased resource inequality and competition over resources such as water or land, potentially resulting in conflict. In Darfur, for example, desertification, land degradation and deforestation have exacerbated the effects of recurrent droughts on communities and have contributed to tensions between nomadic pastoralists and farmers over increasingly scarce pastures, arable soil and fresh water.[20] Current research, however, suggests that although environmental stresses or unmanaged movement of people may contribute to and exacerbate pre-existing tensions, it is not a simple cause-and-effect relationship. Empirical evidence does not support the view that environmental change automatically creates mass migration, which would in turn spur violent conflicts. Much depends on the local context.

Population growth, poverty and systems of governance also influence how environmental change affects people's lives and livelihoods. The twin concepts of "carrying capacity" and "caring capacity" are relevant too. Carrying capacity refers to the particular characteristics of an ecosystem that affect how it sustains human activity or how it becomes vulnerable to the negative effects of climate change. Caring capacity describes the social, developmental and institutional variables that underpin the ability of institutions to cope with environmental stresses.[21] The potential adverse effects of climate change are likely to be especially severe in countries that have both limited carrying and caring capacities.[22]

Move or stay?

The decision to move or stay is usually made at the individual or household levels, especially when gradual environmental degradation is the problem. Therefore, an analysis of how individuals, households and, in some cases, communities respond to environmental change provides insights into when migration is likely, who is likely to migrate and why.

Decisions to migrate are complex and depend on many considerations, including the interplay between carrying and caring capacities. Isolating environmental and especially climate change-related factors from other reasons for migration is therefore difficult in theory and practice. Within any given set of social and environmental circumstances, decisions to move or stay depend on incomes, social networks, local patterns of gender relations and the perceived alternatives to moving. Therefore, just as the environment is only one among many factors that drive migration, migration is only one among many possible responses to environmental change.

Meanwhile, the distinction between voluntary and forced migration is sometimes blurred, further complicating efforts to determine whether or when people will leave their homes because of climate-related circumstances. With the exception of natural disasters that provoke flight in the moment of occurrence, it is usually an accumulation of economic, social and political factors that leads an individual to a decision to move. Through a progressive worsening of conditions, a tipping point may be reached: the decision to move may not be forced, but may also no longer be voluntary. On one end of the continuum are clear cases of forced migration. On the other are clear cases of voluntary migration. A large grey area exists in between the two.

Unequal impacts

Climate change tends to exacerbate differences among various groups, in terms of vulnerability and ability to cope with the effects. In general, vulnerable and socially marginalized groups, such as the poor, children, women, the elderly, and indigenous peoples, tend to bear the brunt of environmental change. It is therefore essential to mainstream considerations of gender, age and diversity into the analysis of climate-change consequences and to focus policy responses on these groups.

Because migration requires economic and other resources, it is a coping strategy not available to everyone. Women, children and the elderly are usually the ones who stay behind, while younger male members are more likely to leave home. Remaining members of the household, particularly women, may therefore become even more vulnerable since they may have to shoulder the burden of caring for the household while having access to fewer income-earning opportunities. In Senegal's Tambacounda region, for example, 90 per cent of the men between the ages of 30 and 60 have migrated at least once in their lifetime. This migration has increased the economic burden on the remaining women and children.[23]

In some cases, out-migration of males may also increase women's vulnerability to the effects of natural disasters, and there is evidence that vulnerability to such disasters differs between men and women. Statistically, natural disasters kill more women than men, or kill women at a younger age than men. In 1991, for example, a cyclone in Bangladesh resulted in five times more deaths of women than men.[24] The differences in death rates between men and women in natural disasters are directly linked to the differences in socio-economic status between the sexes and the degree to which women enjoy economic and social rights. Low socio-economic status of women correlates with larger differences in death rates. Restrictions on behaviour and limited access to information and resources can directly reduce women's chances of survival during a natural disaster or in its aftermath. In addition, because women are the main care givers in many societies, they tend to look after their children's safety at the expense of their own in a crisis.

In addition, because women are disproportionately involved in subsistence farming, natural-resource management and water collection in developing countries, they are more likely to be affected than men by the effects of soil erosion, desertification, droughts, water shortages, floods and other environmental changes.[25]

Both in gradual and sudden migration and displacement scenarios, pre-existing patterns of discrimination and abuse are often aggravated. Women and girls are at risk to sexual and gender-based violence, human trafficking,

Climate change tends to exacerbate differences among various groups, in terms of vulnerability and ability to cope with the effects. In general, vulnerable and socially marginalized groups, such as the poor, children, women, the elderly, and indigenous peoples, tend to bear the brunt of environmental change.

child abuse and alcohol-related abuse. Displaced and refugee women and girls face more dangers in conventional camp and urban settings when gathering firewood, water and seeking livelihoods. In many societies, women are at a further disadvantage when trying to obtain documentation or regain ownership of property.

Furthermore in the context of forced displacement, disasters and crisis, the capacities of health-care systems to respond to increased needs of affected populations are often disrupted or weakened. Because there may be multiple competing health priorities during an emergency, there is a danger that the supply of reproductive health services for women and girls may not meet demand.[26] In general, population displacements increase the health risks for the most vulnerable populations, including pregnant women, the elderly and people with disabilities.

The poor, other marginalized groups and people living in densely populated cities in deltas around the world are particularly vulnerable to climate disasters and slow-onset environmental degradation. The poor often live in slums and in the outskirts of these cities, with limited access to infrastructure, health care and other services. Migration to cities from environmentally degraded rural areas or from areas stricken by natural disasters may exacerbate slum conditions. Dhaka, Bangladesh's capital, on the banks of the Buriganga River, is the world's fastest-growing mega-city with a population of more than 12 million people—double the number of a decade ago—and is projected to grow to 20 million by 2020.[27] Dhaka's slum population, estimated at 3.4 million, is also expected to grow, with as many as 400,000 migrants, most of them poor, arriving each year from rural and coastal areas where environmental hardship is increasingly common.[28]

Because of inadequate absorptive capacity of many of the world's cities and the lack of planning for future growth, rural-to-urban migrants often have no choice but to overexploit or pollute natural resources to meet basic needs. In the absence of affordable housing, migrants may resort to unregulated construction, as well as unsustainable livelihoods and unsanitary practices leading to serious public health risks and degraded land, which exacerbates the effects of and vulnerability to mudslides and floods.[29]

The other side of environmental migration

Not all the news about environmentally induced migration is bad. In some cases, environmentally induced population movements have benefited individuals and communities. Returning migrants may bring with them

---

 TEMPORARY MIGRATION PROGRAMME BENEFITS ENVIRONMENTALLY VULNERABLE COMMUNITIES IN COLOMBIA

Many areas of Colombia are vulnerable to seasonal environmental risks, including water scarcities, floods and soil erosion. In February 2009, for example, the Mira River overflowed its banks, affecting more than 30,000 people.

Environmental vulnerabilities aggravated by climate change are also exacerbated by poverty. These factors, along with conflict and security issues, drive internal and international population movements. An estimated 3.3 million Colombians have moved to other countries, and their remittances to Colombia totalled $4.6 billion in 2007 alone.

Recognizing the potential contribution of migration to development and adaptation to climate change, Colombia established a programme in 2006 that facilitates temporary, seasonal migration to Spain. Originally, the programme aimed to help households whose livelihoods were lost after a volcano erupted in the Galeras region. Since then, however, the programme has been expanded to include people in rural communities where crops and land are vulnerable to floods and other natural disasters.

In Spain, migrants earn an income, mostly through agricultural work, which helps them cover family health-care costs, children's education and housing, and enables women and men to invest in projects for the benefit of their home communities. Migrants also acquire new skills, which can help them diversify their incomes when they return to Colombia.

The programme, supported by the European Union, allows Colombians to increase their resilience to environmental challenges and offers them an alternative to permanent relocation. The recurring six-month placements provide ample time for ecologically fragile land to recover so that marketable crops may again be grown on them.

newly acquired skills and know-how, creating new opportunities for livelihoods and potentially boosting the local economy.[30] Mobility may therefore contribute to the adaptation of people affected by environmental change. Conversely, immobility may increase people's vulnerability to environmental pressures.

According to Cecilia Tacoli of the International Institute for Environment and Development, underlying many of the predictions of hundreds of millions of "climate refugees" and "climate migrants" are the views that migration reflects a failure to adapt to changes in the physical environment and that migrants are a relatively undifferentiated group, all responding similarly to emergencies and moving to unspecified destinations. This view is at odds with a more nuanced and realistic view that migration is an adaptive response to socio-economic, cultural and environmental change. There is growing evidence that mobility, in conjunction with income diversification, is an important strategy to reduce vulnerability to environmental and other risks. In many cases, mobility not only increases resilience to climate change but also enables individuals and households to accumulate assets. Policies that support and accommodate mobility and migration are important for both adaptation and the achievement of broader development goals.[31]

The way forward

No one knows for sure how many people will be on the move as a result of insidious environmental decline or hurricanes, cyclones and other climate-related natural disasters in the decades ahead. Whether the total is 50 million or 1 billion, the international community must be prepared for an increasing number of people temporarily or permanently leaving their homes.

Relief organizations, policymakers, donors, host nations and affected countries themselves are ill-equipped for environmentally induced population movements, partly because of a shortage of credible data and forecasts, which are essential for raising awareness and mobilizing the political will and resources needed to tackle emerging challenges. Furthermore, a better understanding of the impact of environmental factors on population movements and distribution, as well as more detailed and gender-sensitive information on which areas and populations will be

affected most, are urgently needed to effectively plan for, adapt to and mitigate the impacts of climate change on human mobility.[32] This will require not only interdisciplinary research but also multi-stakeholder collaboration in the development of comprehensive approaches.

National and international policies are needed to address environmentally induced population movements. National Adaptation Programmes of Action do not yet include provisions for migration, and national migration management policies do not yet incorporate environment and climate-change considerations. Similarly, the United Nations Framework Convention for Climate Change does not yet consider the implications for climate change on human mobility.

The effectiveness of efforts to mitigate and adapt to the impacts of climate change will depend on the full participation and contribution of women and girls. Improving women's engagement is not only instrumental to reducing their vulnerability but may also significantly contribute to whole communities' survival. The success of adaptation strategies will also depend on the participation of indigenous peoples. Learning from the rich experience of the indigenous peoples, building on the local resources and knowledge to design the appropriate adaptation solutions, has often proved to be the most successful way to increase the resilience of affected populations. Engagement of indigenous people in decision-making about adaptation strategies is also important because these communities are among those most profoundly affected by climate change: their identities are closely linked to their traditional territories and livelihoods, both of which may be threatened by the impact of climate change, which could drive them from their homes.

Migration can be an effective way to adapt to the effects of climate change. Unplanned, sudden migration in response to a natural disaster, however, is likely to set in motion a chain of events which may result in new or additional hardships, including conflict, poverty and further environmental decline. Comprehensive research—including mapping and geographic information system surveys—could provide some of the tools needed to avert or reduce the likelihood of catastrophic upheavals of vulnerable communities, leaving migration a matter of choice rather than necessity and survival itself.

4 Building resilience

"Adaptation is more than a destination; it is a journey, dynamic and continuous, and non-linear. In many countries, populations are coping with climate change, but they are not adapting."

—Sumaya Zakieldeen, Sudanese Environmental Conservation Society[1]

Farmers in Malawi used to be able to predict the coming of the rains, but no longer. So Mazoe Gondwe, the food provider for her family, diversifies production by dividing her plot of land among rain-fed and irrigated crops, hoping for the best.

"But irrigation is back-breaking and can take four hours a day," she told a reporter in late December 2008. Invited by a European non-governmental organization to tell her story at the 14th Conference of the Parties to the United Nations Framework Convention on Climate Change, held in Poznań, Poland, Ms. Gondwe said she needed better irrigation technology to cut the time she spends watering crops. Improved storage facilities and better seed varieties, she added, would be welcome as well.

"As a local farmer, I know what I need and I know what works," she said. "I grew up in the area and I know how the system is changing."[2]

Unfortunately for Ms. Gondwe—and for the rest of us—the climate system will keep changing. Four decades from now, average temperatures in Malawi probably will have risen by at least a full degree Celsius, and agricultural yields will have fallen significantly. Meanwhile, Malawi's population is projected to grow from today's 15 million to as many as 41.5 million in 2050.[3]

The adaptation imperative

Unless some counterbalancing force beyond any current scientific understanding intervenes, the built-in momen-tum of the climate system means that temperatures are likely to rise for decades. The world needs to prepare now for a warming world, even if we cannot predict with any confidence how fast it will heat up—or when and where the heating will end. And while no scientist can assure us that any particular extreme weather event

20 EXTREME WEATHER, POOR RESPONSES

According to a report published in 2009 by Oxfam International, the year 2007 "saw floods in 23 African and 11 Asian countries that were the worst in decades. Two hurricanes and heavy rains hit much of Central America; almost half the state of Tabasco in Mexico was flooded. As the United Nations Emergency Relief Coordinator John Holmes put it: '…all these events on their own didn't have massive death tolls, but if you add [them] together you get a mega-disaster.' But 2008 offered no let-up in the barrage of climatic disasters, as Cyclone Nargis devastated large parts of Myanmar, and a particularly destructive Atlantic hurricane season caused hundreds of deaths and massive economic damage across Cuba, the Dominican Republic, Haiti, and the United States. In many cases, failures in environmental management increased the impact of these climate hazards. In India, the 2008 rains caused serious flooding, not because they were particularly heavy, but because of the failure of poorly maintained dams and river banks. A breach in the Kosi river embankment in August 2008 led to one of the worst floods in the history of Bihar, the poorest state in India."[4]

◄ *Two women negotiate flood water in the Moroccan town of Souk Larbaa.*
© AFP

Figure 4.1: Impact of climate change and the Millennium Development Goals

Millennium Development Goal	Potential impacts of climate change
Goal 1 Eradicate extreme poverty and hunger	• Damage to livelihood assets, including homes, water supply, health and infrastructure, can undermine peoples' ability to earn a living; • Reduction of crop yields affects food security; • Changes in natural systems and resources, infrastructure and labour productivity may reduce income opportunities and affect economic growth; • Social tensions over resource use can lead to conflict, destabilising lives and livelihoods and forcing communities to migrate.
Goal 2 Achieve universal primary education	• Loss of livelihood assets and natural disasters reduce opportunities for full time education, more children (especially girls) are likely to be taken out of school to help fetch water, earn an income or care for ill family members; • Malnourishment and illness reduces school attendance and the ability of children to learn when they are in class; • Displacement and migration can reduce access to education.
Goal 3 Promote gender equality and empower women	• Exacerbation of gender inequality as women depend more on the natural environment for their livelihoods, including agricultural production. This may lead to increasingly poor health and less time to engage in decision making and earning additional income; • Women and girls are typically the ones to care for the home and fetch water, fodder, firewood, and often food. During times of climate stress, they must cope with fewer resources and a greater workload; • Female headed households with few assets are particularly affected by climate related disasters.
Goal 4 Reduce child mortality	• Deaths and illness due to heatwaves, floods, droughts and hurricanes; • Children and pregnant women are particularly susceptible to vector-borne diseases (e.g., malaria and dengue fever) and water-borne diseases (e.g., cholera and dysentery) which may increase and/or spread to new areas; • Reduced water and food security negatively affect child health.
Goal 5 Improve maternal health	• Reduction in the quality and quantity of drinking water has negative effects on maternal health; • Food insecurity leads to increased malnutrition; • Floods and droughts spread water-borne illnes, impacting maternal health.
Goal 6 Combat HIV/AIDS, malaria and other diseases	• Water stress and warmer conditions increase vulnerability to disease; • Households affected by AIDS have lower livelihood assets, and malnutrition accelerates the negative effects of the disease.
Goal 7 Ensure environmental sustainability	• Alterations and possible irreversible damage in the quality and productivity of ecosystems and natural resources; • Decrease in biodiversity and worsening of existing environmental degradation; • Alterations in ecosystem-human interfaces and interactions lead to loss of biodiversity and loss of basic support systems for the livelihood of many people, particularly in Africa.
Goal 8 Develop a global partnership for development	• Climate change is a global issue and a global challenge: responses require global cooperation, especially to help developing countries adapt to the adverse effects of climate change; • International relations may be strained by climate impacts.

Source: *United Nations Framework Convention on Climate Change. 2007. Climate Change: Impacts, Vulnerabilities and Adaptation in Developing Countries. Bonn: United Nations Framework Convention on Climate Change Secretariat. United Nations Development Programme. 2009. Climate Change Affects All the MDGs. At undp.org/climatechange/about.htm.*

is the direct result of human-induced climate change, the pattern of such events suggests a trend and resembles what scientists are expecting for the coming decades. Because the atmosphere has already changed, any weather we experience today has some element, however indiscernible, of human influence.

The "central" range of likely temperature increases in the coming century—2 degrees or 4.5 degrees Celsius—is worrisome enough.[5] More troubling still is the possibility of truly catastrophic temperature increases and climate impacts, especially if Governments do not act decisively and soon to limit emissions. The sea level could rise over the long term by one metre and perhaps significantly more, swamping portions of cities located close to current sea levels along seacoasts and tidal rivers. A 2007 study showed that low-elevation coastal zones—those that are less than 10 metres above sea level—are home to 13 per cent of the world's urban population.[6] Among the world's large cities at risk are Dhaka, Jakarta, Mumbai, New York, Shanghai and Tokyo.[7] Region-wide heat waves unlike any that human beings have ever known could bake cities already turned into "urban heat islands" by massed pavement and concrete. Considering the setbacks to health, development and human life itself that such changes imply, Governments and societies need urgently to plan now for how civilization can withstand such changes and survive.

Until recently the science of climate change has been mostly that: science. We are only beginning to think about the human impacts and the full implications of the various scenarios of climate change promulgated by the Intergovernmental Panel on Climate Change and other scientific bodies. One message, however, emerges from history and recent experience: when conditions are harsh and resources scarce, the poor and groups marginalized by more than poverty—women, the young, the elderly, indigenous peoples and other minorities—are most vulnerable. They are also least often supported and often excluded from participating in societies' collective responses to adversity.

The United Nations and the world's Governments have prioritized a set of goals to be achieved by 2015—the Millennium Development Goals, or MDGs—that, if achieved, would contribute significantly to climate resilience. In an illustration of cycles of causality that can be either virtuous or vicious, however, the MDGs themselves are undermined by early impacts of climate change as well as by population dynamics and consumption patterns. Integration of the MDGs with concerns about climate change, and with efforts to improve access to reproduc-

---

21 REPRODUCTIVE HEALTH, POPULATION AND THE MILLENNIUM DEVELOPMENT GOALS

Each of the MDGs has demographic components or implications related to the human scale of the problems to be addressed and, in many cases, the steps that can be taken to resolve them. The goals cannot be achieved, former United Nations Secretary-General Kofi Annan noted in 2002, "if questions of population and reproductive health are not squarely addressed. And that means stronger efforts to promote women's rights, and greater investment in education and health, including reproductive health and family planning."[8]

In brief, when women can manage the size of their families and the timing of their own childbearing, they are more likely to move toward gender equality, and gender equality itself supports their capacity to manage their reproduction (MDG 3). The use of voluntary family planning directly decreases child mortality (MDG 4) and improves maternal health (MDG 5). The slower population growth that results from access to reproductive health contributes to the eradication of hunger (MDG 1) and makes it less likely that sheer numbers will undermine improvement in school enrollment and the quality of education (MDG 2). Prevention of sexually transmitted infections is a core component of reproductive health, directly contributing to efforts to reduce HIV transmission, while family planning can help HIV-positive women decide for themselves when and whether to bear children, hence reducing mother-to-child transmission (MDG 6).

From the standpoint of MDG 7 on ensuring environmental sustainability, slower population growth operates on multiple fronts—easing increases in water shortages; slowing loss of forests, fisheries and biodiversity; and helping to brake the rise of greenhouse-gas emissions and to build the resilience of countries as they adapt to climate change.

tive health and to achieve gender equality, is all the more vital because progress toward most of the MDGs has been slow. MDG 5—to improve maternal health—is especially behind schedule, with maternal mortality at the same high rate today as two decades ago.[9]

Not all that changes is climate

It is no accident that the developed countries are considered most able to adapt to the impacts of climate change. Societies' *resilience*—the assets, capacity and flexibility that enable them to withstand and adapt to rapid change of all kinds without significant loss of life, health and well-being—in many ways resembles the economic and social endpoint toward which development itself points. This resemblance has actually complicated climate negotiations, with some non-governmental organizations and developing-country Governments worrying that new financing for climate-change adaptation might simply result in reductions in development assistance, trading a shift in nomenclature for real increases in financial flows. "Additionality" for such funds—that they supplement rather than replace development assistance—is a key requirement for equity in any final climate agreement.

The uncertainty about what is climate-change adaptation and what is development is mirrored in the uncertainty about which changes are the impact of climate change and which are environmental phenomena that might well occur even if greenhouse gases had no effect on climate or ecosystems. The distinction is especially important because the United Nations Framework Convention on Climate Change requires those countries most responsible for causing climate change to take the greatest responsibility, subject to their capacity, for addressing the impacts of the problem. Those countries most responsible for the accumulation of excess greenhouse gases in the atmosphere will probably be least devastated by the impacts of climate change, and vice versa.

Given the imbalance between causes and effects and their origins in wealthier and poorer countries, a major objective of an equitable climate agreement to supplement the United Nations Framework Convention on Climate Change and the Kyoto Protocol is to establish new and additional funding mechanisms to help developing nations address the burden placed on them by climate change.

Responsibility for our actions as nations and individuals matters. But trying to assess blame in each case for interconnected environmental, social and economic problems can turn into a limitless distraction from

---

22   CLIMATE CHANGE OR ENVIRONMENTAL DECLINE?

The distinction between the effects of climate change and symptoms of environmental decline may be blurred.

There has always been natural variability in weather. Droughts, storms and heat waves, for example, have occurred with some regularity in many parts of the world over the millennia.

But because of climate change, many of these common weather events are occurring more frequently and with greater severity. Climate change is also melting the polar ice caps, causing sea levels to rise, and bringing protracted drought to parts of the world where dry periods are uncommon.

Recent climate change is primarily the result of the ever-increasing amount of greenhouse gases thrust into the atmosphere, and most of these emissions stem from the burning of fossil fuels. Another major contributor has been deforestation. With fewer and fewer forests, the earth's capacity to absorb excess carbon from the atmosphere is diminished.

Some environmental problems may be mistaken for climate change. For example, farm land sometimes becomes unusable because of salinization that is occasionally the result of rising seas. But salinization of soil is more likely to be the result of irriga-

tion systems that draw the earth's natural salt to the surface. Drying lakes and rivers may be the result of drought, but they may also be the result of excessive use of water for agriculture, industry and people living in nearby metropolises.

Loss of biodiversity is an environmental problem that is in some cases related to climate change, but in other cases is the effect of changing land-use patterns, the demise of forests or pollution. Climate change warms and acidifies the earth's seas, contributing to the death of marine life. But overfishing and pollution also play a role in decline of fish populations in many areas.

the essential task: rapidly evolving effective coopera-tive and cross-cultural responses to the predicaments of a populous, inequitable, gender-divided and generally human-stressed world.

Consideration of population and its interactions with development and the environment is important to the process, not just because of population's long-term contribution to the scale of greenhouse-gas emissions, but because population dynamics interact with and con-tribute to many of the same environmental changes often seen as impacts of climate change. Areas with high rates of population growth are likely to face particular chal-lenges in overcoming food insecurity, Intergovernmental

Panel on Climate Change authors have noted, while changes in climate "will add to the dual challenge of meeting food (cereal) demand while at the same time protecting natural resources and improving environmen-tal quality in these regions."[10]

The availability of renewable fresh water (critical to achievement of MDG 1) is one area that is acutely sensi-tive to population size and growth, as well to levels of economic development. Researchers with the United Nations Department of Economic and Social Affairs recently examined projected trends in rainfall and popu-lation density in Africa between 2000 and 2050 and concluded that demographic change will likely matter

Figure 4.2: The unequal burden

While the developed countries have contributed the most to human-induced climate change up to now (upper world map scaled to fossil-fuel carbon-dioxide emissions in 2002), people in poor countries—most dramatically in Africa—already are much more likely to die as a result of the climate change that occurred up to 2000 (lower world map scaled by the World Health Organization's regional estimates of per capita mortality from late 20th century climate change).

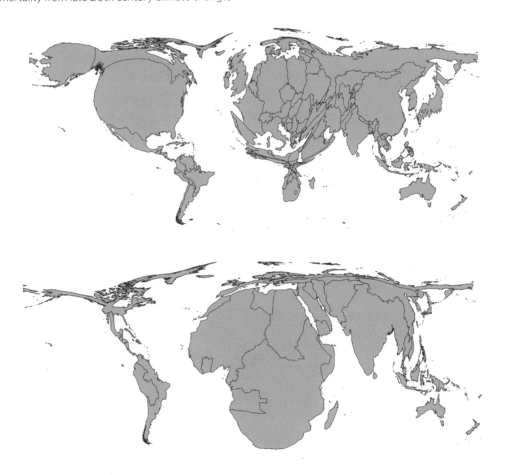

Source: *Patz, J. and others. 2007. "Climate Change and Global Health: Quantifying a Growing Ethical Crisis."* Ecohealth 4:397-405; *World Health Organization. 2008.* Protecting Health from Climate Change: World Health Day 2008. *Geneva: World Health Organization.*

▲ A Bangladeshi woman plants gourds on the roof of her home. The rooftop garden provides food during floods, when waters destroy field crops.
© GMB Akash/Panos Pictures

more than climate change in determining future water availability. Moreover, they noted, slowing population growth can directly contribute to adaptation. "In Southern Africa," the researchers noted, "demographic stagnation [i.e. slow or no population growth], is likely to mitigate significantly the impact of climate change.""

Such conclusions do not suggest any nullification of developed countries' obligations under the United Nations Framework Convention on Climate Change. These obligations include reducing their own greenhouse-gas emissions and providing needed financing and technology transfer to developing countries that are additional to existing development assistance. Similarly, any demographic contributions to social resilience do not suggest any departure from the rights-based approach to population on which the world's nations agreed at the International Conference on Population and Development (ICPD). What they do suggest is the need for a more holistic view, which includes access to reproductive health and gender equality, not only for the long-term reduction of greenhouse-gas emissions but also for the capacity of all nations to adapt to climate change. Even experts sometimes fail to distinguish between the

effects of climate change, global in its origins, and environmental degradation, which may be more the product of local human demand, arising from economic development and population growth.

At the level of communities and the people who live in them, however, the distinction is frequently understood and expressed. Rural women—closer than men to natural resources in direct proportion to their poverty—are often well aware that the actions of their own community or even their own actions can cause local environmental degradation. [12] In Dakar in 2008, women participating in a workshop on climate change and gender from Senegal and Ghana remarked on visible environmental damage stemming from overfishing, illegal net use and, in one case, the collection of seashells by women for microfinance livelihood projects. The participants assessed these points positively, as opportunities for self-education and building awareness of the environmental implications of everyday behaviour. [13] Gender equality and access to reproductive health are central to building and sustaining societies' resilience to the stresses of a warming world. Standing shoulder-to-shoulder with men in all spheres of life and having freedom and power to make reproductive decisions increase women's resilience and help unleash social and economic potential. Equal rights and opportunities for women also usually result in smaller families, thus contributing to long-term population stabilization.

Social and cultural aspects of vulnerability and adaptation

Marginalization of and discrimination against women and the lack of attention to the ways gender inequality hampers development, health, equity and overall human well-being all undermine countries' resilience to climate change. Resilience is most likely to bloom and grow in societies in which all people can go to school, access health services, enjoy equal protection of law, and participate fully in directing their own lives and the destinies of their communities and nations. Often, as well, resilience has its own roots in culture, as in the many cases of traditions of generosity to those in need and cooperative work in the face of calamity.

By their numbers and the inequality of gender relations worldwide, women are most at a disadvantage in navigating and surviving the sorts of stresses— from chronic food insecurity and water scarcity to natural disasters and violent conflict— likely to increase as the planet heats up. While women represent half the world's adult population, by general consensus they constitute a much larger proportion of its poor. Differential gender poverty is not yet fully understood, but there appear to be several factors driving it. In most societies, women work less often for pay than men and receive, on average, less pay for comparable work. In addition, many women in marriages or other unions with men who have low incomes experience "secondary poverty": their partners devote high proportions of their limited income to personal expenditures such as alcohol, drugs and gambling rather than on the family. Finally, single-parent households are far more likely to be headed by women than by men, and the majority of these female-headed households tend to

Women die in greater numbers in disasters than men, and they tend to die at younger ages, but there are few reliable data to document these phenomena, largely because there has so far been little focus by the international community on the gender impact of natural disasters.

be poor. In Bangladesh, for example, as many as three in 10 households are headed by females, and 95 per cent of these female-headed households are below the poverty line.[14] The impacts of women's higher poverty rates and social expectations about their behaviour are especially obvious in the recent history of the onset and aftermath of natural disasters. While many disasters are unrelated to climate change (See Box 4: What do tsunamis have to do with climate change?), the behaviour patterns and outcomes that these disasters manifest may predict patterns and outcomes likely to emerge from climate change to come—unless, that is, we act immediately to create new patterns of inclusion, equity and gender equality.

Women die in greater numbers in disasters than men, and they tend to die at younger ages, but there are few reliable data to document these phenomena, largely because there has so far been little focus by the international community on the gender impact of natural disasters. Localized case studies associated with a devastating 1991 cyclone in Bangladesh, the 2003 European heat wave, and the 2004 Asian tsunami nonetheless affirm the greater vulnerability of women. Sampling data from natural disasters in 141 countries between 1981 and 2002, economists Eric Neumayer and Thomas Plümper confirmed that "natural disasters (and their subsequent impact) on average kill more women than men or kill women at an earlier age than men." Moreover, the researchers found that the more severe the disaster and the lower the socioeconomic status of the population affected, the greater the gap between women's and men's death rates in such disasters as cyclones, earthquakes and tsunamis.

Why are women more vulnerable? No doubt some vulnerability stems from biological differences. A proportion of women in any population will be pregnant, for example, and less able to tolerate the exertion required to escape or survive disasters. Men's greater upper-body muscular mass, on average, may confer advantages in such circumstances. But most of women's heightened vulnerability, Neumayer and Plümper concluded, stemmed not from biology but from society. "Our results show," they wrote, "that it is the socially constructed gender-specific vulnerability of females built into everyday socioeconomic patterns that lead to the relatively higher female disaster mortality rates compared to men."[15]

The accounts of recent disasters, such as the 2004 tsunami, are filled with examples. Many women perished because they were in their homes, unaware of the fateful oncoming wave, while the crest buoyed the boats of their fisherman husbands, who survived. Some women were weighed down by their *saris* and drowned. And still others had never been encouraged to learn to swim despite living all their lives next to water. Girls drowned because they never learned to climb trees as their brothers had. One girl was released into a tidal surge by her father because he could not hold on both to her and to her brother, and, as he said later, the "son has to carry on the family line."[16]

The social vulnerability of women scarcely recedes with the floodwaters. The tensions associated with dealing with catastrophe often exacerbate the risk of gender-based violence that was already present before disaster struck.[17] Around the world, with most Government offices staffed by men and the entrenched assumption that households

have male heads, women often miss out on recovery payments and other assistance. With weaker social networks in the world outside their homes, information essential to survival may pass right by them.

While such post-disaster gendered exclusion has proliferated, awareness of the needs of women has improved among many governmental agencies and non-governmental organizations. At the grass roots, women have simply stepped forward in some cases to insist on participating in disaster management and reconstruction planning. As early as a disastrous 1992 flood in the Sarghoda district of Pakistan, women helped design new housing for their families and became joint owners of the resulting homes, promoting their empowerment. After a 1999 cyclone in Orissa, India, most relief efforts were channeled through women, who received relief supplies, loans and house-building grants, with documented improvement in self-esteem and social status.[18]

Non-governmental organizations have documented inspiring models of women and men working against stereotype. Widower fathers in the wake of disasters sometimes become active caretakers of their children and even move their homes to be close to the children's

 23 **AFTER DISASTER, HYGIENE KITS AND COUNSELLING ON SEXUAL VIOLENCE**

In the year that followed the deadly tsunami of 2004, UNFPA offices in Indonesia, Sri Lanka, Maldives and Thailand coordinated with other United Nations agencies to help in post-disaster reconstruction. UNFPA staff made sure the reproductive and maternal health needs of women and adolescents were not lost amidst the rebuilding and that recovery plans included steps to prevent sexual violence.

In tsunami-affected provinces of Indonesia, primary health centres gained ambulances and instruments for emergency obstetric care, a particular need for pregnant women in communities made even more remote by the aftermath of disaster. Working with the Indonesian Psychologists Association, UNFPA facili-

tated outreach at community centres and trained counsellors in how to respond to gender-based and sexual violence.

Throughout the affected region, UNFPA distributed hundreds of thousands of personal hygiene kits containing—in addition to such basic items as soap, toilet paper, toothbrushes and sanitary napkins—condoms for the prevention of HIV and other sexually transmitted infection as well as unwanted pregnancy. Other reproductive health equipment and supplies used in the post-tsunami response included emergency contraception, safe delivery materials and drugs for the treatment of sexually transmitted diseases.[20]

Over the past decade UNFPA has developed an emergency-response

capacity to deliver essential reproductive health services to those recovering from disasters or living in refugee camps. Such interventions produce long-term benefits for affected populations. One study found that reproductive health indicators such as maternal and infant mortality rates and levels of contraceptive prevalence were higher among refugee populations in Africa than among surrounding populations.[21] There may be a lesson here applicable to the changes expected in a warming world. With sufficient funding and political commitment, such interventions could be universal rather than targeted, helping populations around the world reduce their vulnerability to the impacts of climate change.

schools. Some compensation programmes reward men financially for abstaining from alcohol during post-disaster recovery, successfully easing women's secondary poverty and their vulnerability to spousal abuse.[19]

Climate change and conflict

An emerging fear within the United Nations and among Governments is the possibility that climate change will add to the factors already spur-ring violent civil conflicts in weaker states around the world. (These are variously categorized in research literature as "fragile" or "failed" states, defined as those whose Governments are unable to guarantee security outside of capi-tal cities, and sometimes not even there.) Such states comprise 9 per cent of world population but more than a quarter of the world's poor, exacerbating the likelihood and impact of both gender discrimina-tion and inadequate access to reproductive health.[22]

Although the links between environmental deteriora-tion and civil conflict are debated, security experts agree that scarcities of fresh water and fertile cropland can exacerbate pre-existing tensions. Under the influence of weak economies, inequities of wealth and power, and ineffective Governments, these can break into violence, often fissuring along ethnic lines. The prospect of popula-tion movements in response to sea-level rises may increase the risk of conflict. The conflict in the Darfur region of Sudan may be one example of violence worsened by the impacts of climate change. Visiting the region in 2006, United Nations Secretary-General Ban Ki-moon called attention to a pattern of declining rainfall in recent years, arguing that climate change was already exacerbating desertification and contributing to tension in the region.[23] The women of Darfur have paid a high price for the vio-lence that has surrounded their villages: rape, other forms of sexual violence, with the risks increasing as they forage for water and fuelwood in this resource-poor region.

In part because of the uncertainties of both how climate change will unfold and how much of current conflict relates to climate or environmental change, some experts have urged caution about attributing too strong a connection between climate change and conflict.[24] But the point still holds: conflict and its ancillary impacts are among those impacts of climate change to which we should apply the precautionary principle and antici-pate even if we cannot predict. Given a long history of disproportionate suffering by women and children, the intersection of gender equality, population and the impacts of climate change deserve further research on these linkages and targeted constructive interventions in areas increasingly prone to violent civil conflict.

Rising seas and the challenge of urbanization

Among the more prominent population dynamics of our era is urbanization, the increase in the proportion of a population liv-ing in cities. Once portrayed as all but hopeless cases of overcrowding and ungovernability, even the largest of the world's cities have come to be seen more recently as centres of creativity and innovation, with the poorest inhabitants often the most innovative—in part, perhaps, because of the necessity of surviving in makeshift housing with poor municipal services, as described in UNFPA's *State of World Population 2007: Unleashing the Potential of Urban Growth.*

In the face of ongoing climate change, such innovation will be increasingly needed. Already one in 10 people lives in a coastal city within a few metres of existing sea levels. Estimates of the population at serious risk of displacement from a metre or two in sea-level rise vary from 384 million to 643 million.[25] Almost all net future population growth is projected to occur in or to gravitate toward cities, imply-ing more than a doubling of urban population and an even greater increase in the number of slum-dwellers by the middle of the century. Under such circumstances, impoverished populations tend to be forced to settle on the only land available—sloping hazardously or barely above normal water level—leaving the poor perpetually

> *Given a long history of disproportionate suffering by women and children, the intersection of gender equality, population and the impacts of climate change deserve further research on these linkages and targeted constructive interventions in areas increasingly prone to violent civil conflict.*

vulnerable to torrential downpours, sliding soils, and flooding. Most of the world's biggest cities sit on or near seacoasts or at the mouths of major rivers, amplifying the likelihood that rising waters will become a damaging fact of life as the century progresses. To varying degrees, cities are beginning to anticipate the likely impacts of climate change, applying geographic information systems and similar technologies to their long-range planning.

The spread of disease

Poor health status can also discriminate against women, who are now more likely than men worldwide to be infected by HIV and are disproportionately affected by malaria. Indeed, malaria—among the infectious diseases considered mostly likely to become more prevalent with global warming, given the likely expansion of temperatures conducive to mosquitoes—is now the biggest killer of pregnant women in sub-Saharan Africa.[26] Dengue fever and various tick-borne diseases are also considered likely either to increase generally or at least shift in prevalence

among regions, as temperatures rise and rainfall patterns change. Research cited in the Intergovernmental Panel on Climate Change's *Fourth Assessment Report* projects diarrheal disease, a scourge among the children of the world's poor, to increase by up to 5 per cent from current levels as early as 2020. As the primary caretakers of children, women will feel the burden of these additions to existing infectious disease.

The health impacts of climate change are particularly uncertain, however. Panel authors assign lower confidence levels to predictions of health impacts than they do to those of sea level rise or more intense storms. One reason is that health and disease respond to so many human factors: nutritional status, the safety of water supplies and sanitation, the quality and extent of health facilities, and the balance of preventive and curative services they offer. Among the largest factors in the spread of infectious diseases such as H1N1, or swine flu, are the rising density of human populations and the ease of air travel in a globalized economy.

Figure 4.3: Cities at low-elevation coastal zones (LECZs)

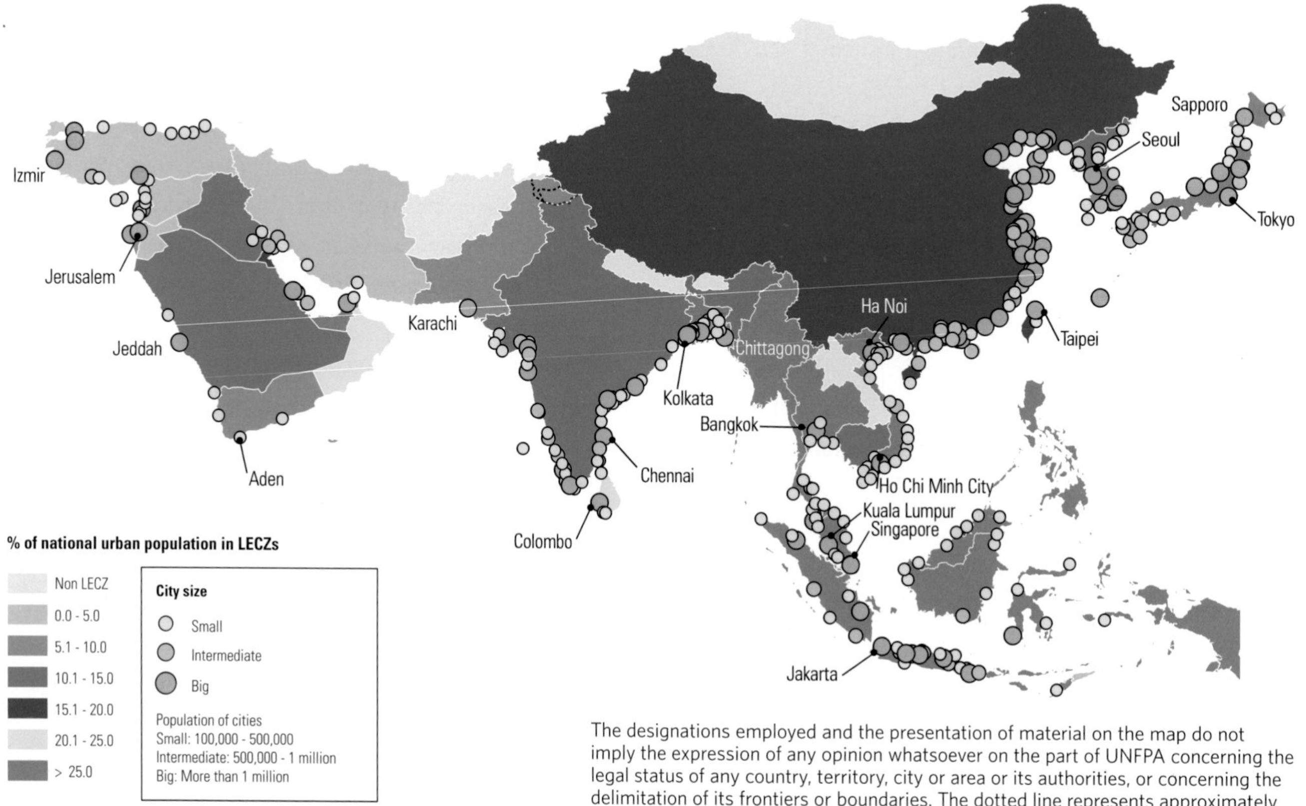

% of national urban population in LECZs

	Non LECZ
	0.0 - 5.0
	5.1 - 10.0
	10.1 - 15.0
	15.1 - 20.0
	20.1 - 25.0
	> 25.0

City size
- Small
- Intermediate
- Big

Population of cities
Small: 100,000 - 500,000
Intermediate: 500,000 - 1 million
Big: More than 1 million

Source: *UN Habitat.*

The designations employed and the presentation of material on the map do not imply the expression of any opinion whatsoever on the part of UNFPA concerning the legal status of any country, territory, city or area or its authorities, or concerning the delimitation of its frontiers or boundaries. The dotted line represents approximately the Line of Control in Jammu and Kashmir agreed upon by India and Pakistan. The final status of Jammu and Kashmir has not yet been agreed upon by the parties.

Health concerns stem not only from the impacts of climate change but its causes as well. Pollution from the same fossil fuels that cause climate change may damage reproduction itself. The Government of China, for example, recently acknowledged increases in birth defects related to pollution, especially the surging combustion of coal powering the country's strong economic growth.[27] A world that shifts from carbon-based to renewable energy sources will undoubtedly experience improved public health.

The rising insecurity of food

Agriculture may be the arena where the well-being of women and their relative invisibility in official statistics are most at odds with the need to build social resilience to climate change. Women produce far more of the world's food than they are given credit for—especially in developing countries—and even today the gap is wide between the resources available to women farmers and their contribution to global food security. Moreover, women farmers are far less likely to own the land they cultivate. Worldwide, according to the International Center for Research on Women, less than 15 per cent of land is

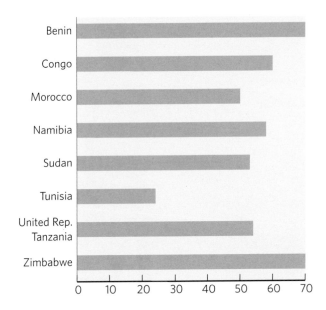

Figure 4.4: The percentage of agricultural work carried out by women in selected countries

Source: *United Nations Environment Programme/GRID Arendal. 2008. Website: http://maps. grida.no/go/graphic/the-percentage-of-agricultural-work-carried-out-by-women-compared-with-the-percentage-of-female-exte, accessed 27 July 2009.*

owned by women. The world is learning how precarious food security can be even when the impacts of climate change are only beginning to be seen. The prospects for food production are especially worrisome in southern Africa, where the most recent Intergovernmental Panel on Climate Change's assessment projects devastating losses in yields, especially for small farmers, absent effective adaptation efforts.[29]

In food as in health, the connections between women's lives, economic development, population and climate run in multiple directions. Among the biggest impacts of climate change on agriculture so far has been the sudden replacement of food crops with crops such as sugarcane and sweet corn, to produce bio-fuels as developed-country Governments mandated partial replacement of petroleum-based vehicle fuels with bio-fuels. At the same time, the forces of economic and demographic growth and global trade have led to a significant increase in the scale of food production, with agribusinesses frequently replacing independent farmers, many of them women. This has been accentuated as most developing countries have invested in the production of cash crops and irrigated farming at the expense of subsistence farming on

 24 **HIV, AIDS AND CLIMATE CHANGE**

The future course of HIV and AIDS will hinge upon societies' capacities to adapt to increases not only in infectious diseases but also food and water shortages, more intense storms, and other climate-change impacts.[28] The success and extent of HIV prevention and AIDS treatment can thus contribute to social resilience against the more diverse threats on the way.

UNAIDS—the Joint United Nations Programme on HIV/AIDS—and the United Nations Environment Programme recently considered how society's approach to the pandemic is likely to influence adaptation to climate change. The two organizations identified main areas of concern: global and regional food security, the distribution of infectious diseases, the influence of governance on conflict and poverty, and the disproportionate impact of HIV and AIDS on young and poor women. Of particular concern was the possibility that climate change could reduce income from such natural resource-intensive activities as farming and fishing, possibly driving some women into sex work and thereby increasing HIV infection rates.

▲ *Bangladeshi women now earn a living from salt-water fishing in areas that have become permanently flooded as a result of rising seas.*
© GMB Akash/Panos Pictures

rain-fed lands. Finally, farmers the world over are facing new and stiff competition for finite freshwater supplies from growing urban areas and the water needs of industry. Shifts in precipitation patterns can only exacerbate stresses on the world's food supply that would be worrisome enough without additional and hard-to-predict threats from climate change.[30]

A world that takes seriously the need to rid the atmosphere of excess carbon dioxide, however, is likely to rediscover the value of farmers who work directly with their soil and crops on land they own and can keep. The world's farmers will need to transform themselves from net emitters of greenhouse gases to net absorbers of carbon dioxide to slow and perhaps reverse the rise of concentrations in the atmosphere. That process will require different agricultural production systems based on boosting the carbon content of soils while reducing the need for chemical fertilizers. Women as well as men who own and improve their own land and food production as climate changes can become the models of the resilience humanity needs. This can be one part of the broader social transition toward health and equality and the envi-

ronmental transition towards sustainable use of resources and balance with the global atmosphere and climate.

Women and resilience

Ultimately, the elements likely to make societies resilient to climate change are probably the same ones that lead to equitable development, full exercise of human rights, social and environmental justice, and an environmentally sustainable world.

Women are doubly limited in their efforts to contribute fully to the societies in which they live. Without adequate social support, reproductive and family roles can limit women's participation in economic, civic and political life. In the Kyrgyz Republic, one-quarter of all women surveyed said their domestic work made it impossible for them to work outside the home. A negligible proportion of men cited such reasons for not working. In rural sub-Saharan Africa, women typically spend from two to six hours per week carrying water from a source within 400 metres of their household.[31] It is not surprising that economic and broader social opportunities are limited under such circumstances.

On top of these constraints, socially conditioned gender roles—the roles of women and men—place limits on what women may pursue and achieve. In a world whose changing climate must be simultaneously combated and adapted to, shackles on half the world's population are unsupportable. A positive develop-ment amidst these constraints is that many women are moving forward despite these constraints. They are modelling new ways of operating in society and relating to one another in ways that could make a difference—not just to climate but to sustainable social relations and a sustainable environment overall.

25 INDIGENOUS WOMEN ADAPTING TO CLIMATE CHANGE

Indigenous peoples—especially indigenous women—remain under-represented in global talks on climate change. But they have a vital contribution to make, says Victoria Tauli-Corpuz. The sustainable, low-carbon lifestyle? Indigenous peoples have lived it for millennia. "Many of the solutions that are being discussed now have always been a way of life for our ancestors and present generations," says Tauli-Corpuz.

A member of the Kankana-ey Igorat peoples of the Philippines, Victoria Tauli-Corpuz is chairperson of the United Nations Permanent Forum on Indigenous Issues and founder and director of Tebtebba, an indigenous people's policy research centre. Tauli-Corpuz fought for—and, ultimately, helped win—the United Nations Declaration on the Rights of Indigenous Peoples, which was adopted by the General Assembly in 2007.

Raised in a village in the Cordillera region of the Phillipines, Tauli-Corpuz came to Manila on a scholarship in the early 1970s and soon became involved in demonstrations against the Vietnam War. She returned home to find that her ancestral lands were threatened by a huge hydroelectric dam project. "We had to organize ourselves to protest the dam project," she says. "So, that's how I started, and I never stopped."

Now Tauli-Corpuz is turning to the issue of climate change, which she sees, fundamentally, as an issue of social justice. Reducing greenhouse-gas emissions is only half the battle; the other half, often neglected, is about promot-ing sustainable, equitable development. Here, indigenous women can play a central role, as they often have respon-sibility for—and valuable knowledge about—sustainable agriculture, forestry, watershed management and more.

Indigenous women are also taking an active role in *adapting* to climate change—by developing crops that are flood- and drought-resistant, protect-ing water resources, and taking care of those sickened by water- and vector-borne diseases that are more prevalent in a warming world.

Different responsibilities mean that indigenous women—and women gen-erally—are affected by climate change in different ways than men. It's impor-tant to understand those differential impacts, says Tauli-Corpuz, because, "if you are not aware of them, the solutions you bring about might not necessarily solve the problems of women."

Tauli-Corpuz learned much about the problems women face while work-

© UN Photo/Paulo Filgueiras

ing in indigenous communities in the Philippines. Trained as a nurse, she saw that reproductive health is a critical component of women's well-being. In indigenous communities where infant and child mortality rates are high, women will often have many children to ensure that some survive. Also, where many hands are needed for subsis-tence farming, indigenous women face great pressure to bear many children. In some cases, women who attempt to control their own fertility are subjected to domestic violence. At the other end of the spectrum, indigenous women in some countries have faced forced steril-ization at the hands of the Government. That's why Tauli-Corpuz has long advo-cated for appropriate family planning services for indigenous women. "It is a problem if you lack family planning ser-vices," she says, "and it is also a problem if they are not the right services."

Tauli-Corpuz believes that reproduc-tive health care is crucial for women, and she believes that it is important to stabilize population. But she disagrees with those who see population growth as a major cause of climate change. "I don't think that's really the main thing," she says. "The main thing is really the lifestyles—the economic development model that's being pushed." Moreover, "if you think population is the problem, and undertake centralized ways of controlling population growth, we will be in an even greater mess." Ultimately, says Tauli-Corpuz, "women have to be the ones to decide how many children they have."

⑤ Mobilizing for change

"Women are important actors in ensuring their communities' ability to cope with and adapt to climate change. They can be effective agents of change and are often the ones turned to in times of need and can play a role in crisis situations."

—The United Nations Framework Convention on Climate Change Secretariat[1]

Working with farming communities along the flood-ravaged coast of southwestern Bangladesh, the humanitarian organization CARE has maximized its employment of women, trained all staff in gender relations, and prioritized work with female-headed households. Some time ago women farmers lamented that their chickens, a profitable source of livelihood when the weather was fair, were drowning when the monsoon season drove floodwaters over the land. The farmers and the non-governmental organization identified a strategy that effectively solved the problem: Give up on chickens. Raise ducks.[2]

This strategy could serve as an epigram for one of the essential tasks the whole world faces—adjusting to and thriving amidst the changes on the way. Successfully carrying out this task will require mobilizing public opinion and political will for mitigating and adapting to climate change. Women in poor and wealthy countries alike are increasingly working either directly on climate change, on the global stage or in their own communities, or they are struggling and strategizing to prevail amid deteriorating environmental conditions. Often men are involved along with women in propelling this work. Those who work on climate change and those who work on reproductive health and rights have much in common and much to learn from each other. To paraphrase Nobel Peace Prize laureate Wangari Maathai of Kenya, there is unlikely to be climate equity without gender equity. And as the world's Governments noted at the International Conference on Population and Development (ICPD), there is unlikely to be gender equity until all women, men and young people have access to a full range of reproductive health services, from voluntary family planning to safe motherhood and the prevention of HIV and other sexually transmitted infections.

The front lines of climate change

Women the world over tend to be more involved in managing energy within the household, while men manage energy at the level of cities and nations. Men often claim technology as their realm. In the early 1990s, solar cookers (stoves using mirrors to concentrate the sun's energy for heating food) failed to catch on in Zimbabwe, for example, in large part because men objected to women learning how to use new devices the men knew nothing about; so, using their power as heads of households, the men refused to buy them.[3]

Yet women overcome such obstacles every day, especially when they work together—and sometimes with men as well as women—toward collective objectives. The fact that women are far more likely than men to repay loans for small-scale entrepreneurial activities is the basis of a global microfinance industry for women's initiatives. The microfinance idea began in Bangladesh with the Grameen Bank and is now an important part of lending at the World Bank and other multilateral finance institutions.

In India, an organization called the Self-Employed Women's Association has 500,000 members in western

◀ *Women in a flood-prone community in Gaibandha, Bangladesh, gather once a week to share ideas about how to adapt to worsening climate and rising seas.*
© GMB Akash/Panos Pictures

Gujarat state alone. Its bank boasts 350,000 depositors, and the repayment rate for its loans has been as high as 97 per cent. "We don't have a liquidity problem," bank manager Jayshree Vyas told a reporter. "Women save."[4]

Many gender discrepancies cross cultures, but at least those related to energy and technology management grow less acute as incomes rise with development, and as women become mass consumers and, often, business managers.[5] As they make this transition, women bring with them perspectives that come in large part from their roles as child-bearers and primary care-givers of new generations. Although gender differences are hotly debated,

in recent years there has been intriguing evidence about the practical benefit of involving women much more fully in enterprises at all levels. The question isn't whether women or men are more resourceful, only whether they bring different perspectives, contributions, and qualities to the table.

"First we thought it would waste our time, because women wouldn't know how to run a village," said a Tanzanian village councilman, asked in 2002 about recent legal changes that brought women into his council. "But we were surprised. The women on the council see things in different ways and come up with ideas none of the rest of us would have thought of. We wouldn't want to lose them now."[6]

26 WANGARI MAATHAI: WOMEN HOLD THE KEYS TO CLIMATE'S FUTURE

"When we started [planting trees] we were not thinking about climate change," Nobel Peace Prize laureate and Green Belt Movement founder Wangari Maathai says, "but it now happens that this work is also extremely important as a way of dealing with the issue."

In the mid-1970s, Maathai partnered with rural women (and some men) around Kenya to rejuvenate the environment by planting trees—more than 40 million to date (the Green Belt Movement has also supported community-based tree-planting efforts in other African countries as well as Haiti.) As landscapes are transformed, so are lives and minds.

Today, the Green Belt Movement is exploring partnerships with the World Bank to plant trees as a way of mitigating the greenhouse-gas emissions fueling climate change. "We want to learn the ropes," Maathai says. "Carbon credits and carbon trading present a new opportunity for the Green Belt Movement to do what it's always done, but now in partnership with organizations and Governments that are now addressing this issue of climate change."

Maathai's biggest concern related to global warming is that poor regions and

communities won't be able to adapt fast enough, in part because they don't have the capital to afford greener, more efficient technologies. What, she asks, "will Governments in Africa or elsewhere do if, for example, the seas rise and people move from coastal areas to the hinterlands in large masses? What will happen in Africa if the desertification process is so enhanced that a huge number of people will have to move to areas where there are greener pastures?"

Why haven't more women been involved to date in global warming negotiations and policy development? Climate change is a "science-based

© Mainichi Corporation

subject," Maathai answers, and continuing gender inequities in women's access to education are the main reason. If women "are not getting adequate education, are not well represented in the sciences, not well represented in decision-making, that will be reflected at the negotiating table," she says.

In developing and implementing climate policy, Maathai sees gender as essential. "Quite obviously, when we talk about reducing emissions from deforestation and degradation, we need to focus on women and we need to focus on communities, particularly communities that live near forests," she says, ensuring that they understand the impacts of climate change and the effects it will have on their livelihoods. Such inclusion is also integral, in Maathai's view, to changing behaviours at the grass roots that can build resilience to global warming, such as reducing forest clearing or degradation, and improving agricultural practices. "That's one level," Maathai says. "The other is the decision-making level that must allocate resources that will ensure that these women and these communities are educated, engaged and guided so they do the right things."

▲ Women near Hyderabad plant crops adaptable to climate change in the bed of a dried-up lake as part of a national rural employment project that will benefit India's environment.
© Reuters

Women marketers of smokeless stoves in India won over women consumers by customizing each unit with special artwork.[7] In the developed world, a 2007 Danish study found companies with a roughly equal balance of women were significantly more innovative and better at developing new products and services as companies without such gender balance.[8]

Women, men and the management of risk

A considerable body of research supports claims that, on average, men and women approach financial and other risks differently: men are somewhat more likely to accept large risks for potentially large gains, while women tend more to eschew extreme risks for lesser ones, even though they typically yield more modest gains.[9] A study in France, for example, concluded that companies that most successfully weathered the 2008 global financial crisis were those with the highest proportion of women in management.[10] The women managers approached risk more conservatively, thus helping avert the large losses experienced by their male counterparts.

Might men's and women's different approaches to risk in general also apply specifically to climate change?

The past few years have seen an upsurge of collective women's enterprises in developed and developing countries alike. And much of that has grown in response either to the challenge of limiting the risks from climate change, or to the need to adapt to hardships stemming at least in part from a changing climate. Women farmers in Malawi are joining together in "farmers' clubs" to share the latest information about seeds and cultivation techniques that can take advantage of poor soils and erratic rainfall.[11] In peri-urban areas of Mali, they form associations and pool resources to purchase or rent small plots of land for gardening.[12] In Bangladesh, some of the poorest and most marginalized women living along rivers opportunistically build temporary dwellings and harvest resources on *chars*, silt islands unburdened by property titles that appear

In the global fight against climate change, says Monique Barbut, one powerful weapon has not been adequately deployed: "the good sense that most women have."

Barbut should know. As the Chief Executive Officer of the Global Environment Facility (GEF), Barbut has brought her trademark good sense to an institution that is now the world's largest funder of efforts to protect the global environment. From that position, Barbut is working to make sure that women play a larger role in efforts to mitigate and adapt to climate change.

Supported by donor countries, the GEF has provided or leveraged more than $40 billion in funding for environmental projects in the developing world since 1991. But, by the time Barbut took its helm in 2006, the GEF had grown into an unwieldy bureaucracy, where projects typically took 66 months to move from conception to implementation. Barbut set out to change that, and succeeded: today, the process takes just 22 months. The transformation was not easy, she says. "When you talk about reforms, everybody applauds you. But when you start to implement them, everybody insults you."

Barbut attributes her success to a certain fearlessness, acquired over years of working in the male-dominated fields of finance and development. Trained as an economist, Barbut began her career at France's economic development bank, la Caisse centrale de coopération économique, before moving to the foreign aid agency, Agence française de développement, and then to the United Nations Environment Programme.

Working among men has given Barbut an appreciation for the particular contributions women bring to the table. Like pragmatism, for example. "Women are very concrete, very pragmatic—they move quickly to solutions, while men

take more time to discuss around the issue," Barbut says. And farsightedness: the experience of mothering, she believes, gives women a special investment in the future.

Women's pragmatism and farsightedness are much needed in the effort to address climate change. At the same time, women in developing countries who live close to nature are often the keepers of ancestral knowledge that may hold solutions to climate challenges. "Not everything has to be high-tech to be good," says Barbut.

© Global Environment Facility

To engage women more fully in the effort to address climate change and other environmental problems, Barbut is working to incorporate a gender perspective in all of the GEF's work. In practical terms, that means analysing the needs of women and men to ensure that women benefit equitably from GEF investments. It also means involving women—consistently—throughout the life of the project. "You don't just have a stakeholder meeting where you invite five women on the first day of the conception of the project, and then forget them," says Barbut.

The best projects tackle environmental problems while markedly improving the lives of women and girls. For example,

investments in public transportation are important—not just to reduce emissions from vehicles—but to connect women to educational, commercial and political opportunities. In many developing countries, where women are not taught to drive, "you need the right transportation if you want them to be part of the society," says Barbut. Similarly, introducing photovoltaics in areas that are not connected to the grid can free up women's time and connect them to the larger world—benefits that Barbut says "go way beyond light and electricity."

Barbut believes that women have much to contribute to solving climate change and other environmental issues, yet she herself came to this field by accident: when she was given the task of representing the Government of France at an international conference on the environment. Barbut decided that her practical experience in finance could make a needed contribution to the field. But her colleagues were mystified: "At that time, it was not very good for your career in finance to say, 'I want to take care of environmental problems.'"

Barbut urges other women to contribute their experience, their expertise and their wisdom to fighting climate change. Although women are appearing in larger numbers at climate negotiations and in other forums, "the number does not make the voice," she says; the conversation is still dominated by men. Her advice to women climate activists: "We should not be afraid to raise good sense propositions, even if they don't look clever. It is much more important to have two feet on the ground."

and just as quickly disappear with shifts in water levels. Perhaps the most vulnerable denizens in that climate-threatened country, these women demonstrate the value of traditional knowledge by managing a changing environment with little or no support from their societies.[13]

Rural women in west-central Nepal are reaching in another direction: toward video technology that can teach them how to communicate their adaptation needs in ways that make a difference. In the aftermath of deadly monsoon floods of 2007, the United Kingdom-based non-governmental organization ActionAid and researchers at Sussex University visited communities lacking basic services and struggling to maintain their agricultural livelihoods despite changes in monsoon and other weather patterns. Dealing mostly with women (because many of the men had migrated from the area to seek other work), ActionAid staff and researchers helped the communities prioritize their needs. Soon the idea emerged to use video cameras to help women dramatize their circumstances and needs and effectively visualize how they could ask local officials for needed resources to better their lives. By the assessments of the British organizations, the exercise has not only improved women's empowerment in the districts but helped the women go beyond adaptation and reach for influence on policy in their communities and beyond.[14]

Policy support, women and climate change

After years of negligible awareness of women in the context of climate change, the international policy community appears to be increasing efforts to acknowledge the influence of gender and to overcome obstacles that hamper women's mitigation and adaptation efforts. The Secretariat of the United Nations Framework Convention on Climate Change is newly committed to taking gender into consideration in its deliberations, and the Global Environment Facility is now committed to assessing the impacts of its investments on women.

Both the science and the policy of climate change have long been and remain dominated by men. Just 16 per cent of the scientists contributing to the work of the Intergovernmental Panel on Climate Change are women, including Susan Solomon of the United States, co-chair of Working Group I, which deals with the science of climate change and is one of three such groups.

Women fare no better among heads of Government climate delegations, however, than they do as contributors to the Intergovernmental Panel on Climate Change's work, with proportions varying from 8 per cent to 18 per cent. The percentage of women at the negotiating tables of the Conferences of the Parties to the United Nations Framework Convention on Climate Change appears to be improving slightly. According to the non-governmental organization GenderCC, it varied from 15 per cent to 23 per cent in the 1990s and in recent years has been around 28 per cent.

These proportions are actually little different than those of women in key decision-making positions generally around the world. Only seven of the world's 150 elected national leaders are women.[15] In national assemblies, women hold just 18.4 per cent of the seats, and only in 22 countries can they claim more than 30 per cent. Progress is detectable, but it is slow. At the current rate of increase, by one calculation, it will be 2045 in most developing countries before neither sex holds more than 60 per cent of parliamentary seats.[16]

In some cases, the best progress in women's participation in climate negotiations can be found in developing countries. Bernaditas Muller is lead climate negotiator of the Philippines and coordinator for the delegations at United Nations climate negotiations of the Group of 77 and China.

Still, strong involvement of or participation by women remains the exception in the climate-change field, and it may continue to be the exception without stronger commitment by Governments and the publics they serve. Indeed, given the universality of the issue and the challenges it presents, climate change science and policy work will benefit from diversity not only in gender but also from diversity in age and income and from the inclusion of indigenous people.

Women and civil society: lessons for climate change

The history of environmental, population and development negotiations outside the climate sphere demonstrates that women's participation can be substantial and influential. The last two decades in particular have seen dramatic growth in "global civil society"—international networks of activists working to protect the environment, secure women's rights, promote sustainable development and more. Fuelled by new awareness that these issues transcend national boundaries—and by the diffusion of low-cost communication technologies and travel—global civil society played a significant part in the major United Nations conferences of the 1990s, especially those on environment (1992), human rights (1993), population (1994) and women (1995).

The growing influence of global civil society has enabled women to play a much larger role in United Nations decision-making, by creating alternative channels to male-dominated national delegations. (In 2000, more than 40 per cent of United Nations delegations consisted of only men, according to the Commission on Sustainable Development Non-governmental Organization Women's Caucus.[18]) Through these new channels, women activists have applied a gender lens to some of the most urgent issues of our time—bringing their perspective and life experiences to bear on the way these issues are understood and addressed.

For example, in the run-up to the 1992 United Nations Conference on Environment and Development (UNCED), women from 83 countries assembled in Miami for the first World Women's Congress for a Healthy Planet, sponsored by the Women's Environment and Development Organization.[19] At that meeting, women from many nations and diverse backgrounds shared life stories of environmental challenges and

28 BERNADITAS MULLER: WOMEN MUST BE EMPOWERED

Climate negotiator Bernaditas Muller is accustomed to being outnumbered by men. A career diplomat, Muller now serves as lead negotiator for the Philippines and as coordinator of delegations from the developing nations' Group of 77 (which now includes many more than 77 countries) and China. But Muller does not see gender as a constraint in the mostly male world of climate negotiations. "If anything," she says, her fellow negotiators are "more polite because I'm a woman."

The big divide on climate change, says Muller, is between the affluent nations of the North and the developing nations of the South. The affluent countries, she says, have not met their legally binding commitments to provide financial resources and technology transfers to developing nations. Moreover, when resources are provided, they are treated by the affluent countries as "development assistance," with many strings attached.

The failure to meet those commitments is symptomatic of a larger unwillingness to accept responsibility for climate change, says Muller. Until 2004, she says, some 75 per cent of the greenhouse gases accumulating

above natural levels in the atmosphere were emitted by developed countries, which account for only 20 per cent of the world's population. So, historically, the 80 per cent of the population that lives in developing countries has contributed just a quarter of all emissions. That lopsided responsibility for creating the problem means that developed and developing countries have differentiated responsibilities for solving it.

Fundamentally, Muller argues, it's about reducing consumption and changing lifestyles that are unsustainable—a responsibility that belongs mostly to the developed countries. "One must bite the bullet," she says. That means, for example, building cities around viable public transportation systems, with neighbourhood schools and shops. It also means rethinking what we buy, wear and eat. "Do we actually need strawberries in winter?"

The importance of changing lifestyles points to a key role for women, says Muller, because—like it or not—women are usually responsible for household work. (Muller is quick to point out that her husband, who enjoys baking cakes, defies the stereotypical

© Climate Change Coordination Centre

gendered division of labour.) Women in affluent countries have substantial power to reduce their families' carbon footprint and environmental impact. At the same time, women in developing countries have the power to reject the consumption pattern modelled on more affluent countries and to craft their own alternatives. And women everywhere have the power to teach the next generation about the importance of sustainability.

For sustainable development to succeed, says Muller, "women must be empowered."

solutions, and produced the Women's Action Agenda 21, a blueprint for incorporating women's concerns into environmental decision-making. At the UNCED conference itself in Rio de Janeiro, the "women's tent"—the largest in the Non-governmental Organization Forum—offered a focal point for networking and strategizing.

The success of these efforts is reflected in the conference document, Agenda 21, which includes more than 145 references to the roles and positions of women in environment and sustainable development, as well as a separate chapter entitled "Global Action for Women towards Sustainable Development."[20] Agenda 21 identifies women as one of the nine "major groups" for implementing its broad programme of action.

Paradigm shifts

The women who took part in UNCED prompted a seismic shift in thinking about environmental policy. They demonstrated that effective policy cannot be "gender neutral." Instead, they showed that it is essential to acknowledge the role of women as stewards of natural

29 CANADA AND CHINA, COOPERATING TO ENGAGE WOMEN

The Canadian International Development Agency is working with the Government of China to reduce carbon emissions in China's paper and pulp, fertilizer, and plastics industries—but with a gender twist to the work. Funded through the Canada Climate Change Development Fund, the Canada-China Cooperation Project in Cleaner Production aims for at least 30 per cent participation of women in the project and to greatly expand their representation among managers, technicians and workers in the industries. Baseline research disaggregated by sex informs the work, and gender equality awareness sessions are designed to develop and incorporate participants' gender analysis into project activities. Women received training in process improvement, auditing practices, monitoring of equipment and computer use. A key objective is to increase women's awareness, abilities, self-confidence and motivation to address the issue of climate change. So enthusiastically have women taken to the project's objectives that they have taken on their own environmental initiatives off the job.[17]

Figure 5.1: Women's share in delegations to Conferences of the Parties to the United Nations Framework Convention on Climate Change

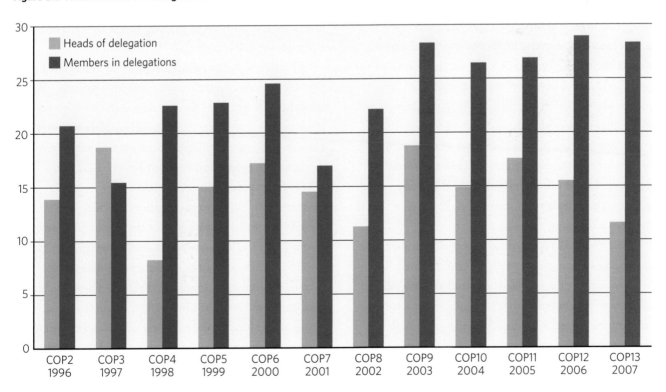

Source: *Lebelo, D. and G. Alber. 2008. "Gender in the Future Climate Regime." Berlin: GenderCC—Women for Climate Justice.*

▲ A woman prepares to plant a seedling during the "Feast of the Forest" in Puerto Princesa, the Philippines. Participants attend the annual event to plant trees in deforested areas to help stem global warming.

© Reuters/John Javellana

resources, because "no one knows the realities of the over-exploitation of the land more intimately than the women who till it, draw and carry its water, use its trees for fuel, harvest forests for healing herbs and medicinal plants, and use their traditional knowledge for the benefit of the community…"[21] These roles and responsibilities render women disproportionately vulnerable to the impacts of environmental degradation, and they also place women at the centre of any meaningful effort to implement solutions. Empowering women, by ensuring access to the resources and information they need to make sound decisions about resource management, is therefore key to sustainable development.

The 1994 ICPD marked another paradigm shift. The Programme of Action that emerged from the event was the culmination of a worldwide effort to shift population policies and programmes from an emphasis on achieving demographic targets for reduced population growth to a focus on improving the reproductive health of populations. Women, together with men, achieved an approach to population policy that is built on a foundation of respect for rights and human development. "All couples and individuals have the basic right to decide freely and responsibly the number and spacing of their children and to have the information, education and means to do so," participating Governments agreed.[22] Empowering women is key: where women have access to education, liveli-hoods, family planning and other health services, they have healthier—and smaller—families, on average later in their own lives than would otherwise be the case.

Since the ICPD, national population policies have evolved in line with the ICPD's Programme of Action. In India, for example, the state family planning programme has abandoned demographic "targets" in favour of free and informed choice in reproductive health services.[23]

Many aspects of the ambitious Programme of Action have been hampered by funding constraints. Since the mid-1990s, funding for reproductive health services, including family planning, has declined as a percentage of health spending and in many cases in real terms as well. As a result, some 200 million women in developing countries have unmet need, lacking access to family planning services and thus unable to exercise their right to make decisions about the number and spacing of their children.[24] The larg-est amount earmarked for family planning since the ICPD was in 1995, with $723 million committed, remaining above $600 million for all but one year to 1999. The latest estimate, for 2007, is about $338 million.[25]

The same kind of paradigm shift that culminated in the ICPD is also needed in the latest international efforts to address climate change. A gender-sensitive approach must replace one where questions of equality between women and men have largely been ignored and where women have been mostly excluded from the debate.

Over the years, efforts to "mainstream" a gender perspective in environmental policy have met with mixed success. In preparation for the World Summit on Sustainable Development in 2002, women's groups reviewed progress towards implementing the gender-specific recommendations in Agenda 21. They concluded that important steps had been taken at international, national and local levels, but these efforts were scattered and most were *ad hoc*. They found no real integration of gender issues into global environment and sustainable development policies and activities, let alone a thorough mainstreaming of gender concerns in these areas.

The United Nations meetings of the 1990s offer important lessons for efforts to incorporate a gender perspective in climate change. First, active involvement by women advocates is essential to produce a gender-sensitive agreement. But, while many organizations are now working to bring a gender perspective to climate issues, women remain underrepresented in the negotiating process.

Women were, however, an increasingly forceful presence at recent Conferences of the Parties to the United Nations Framework Convention on Climate Change in Bali in 2007 and Poznań in 2008. Women-led and women-staffed non-governmental organizations, such as the Women's Environment and Development Organization and GenderCC, worked together with the United Nations Environment Programme and the Global Gender and Climate Alliance, an alliance of civil society and United Nations agencies, to advance a gender agenda in the talks. Climate non-governmental organizations based in developing countries, including

---

30   **MALINI MEHRA: AIMING FOR THE TRIPLE BOTTOM LINE**

When political scientist Malini Mehra looks around during climate conferences in India and in developed countries, she finds "a paucity of women among the bureaucrats and politicians tasked with climate policy." But her message that positive action is needed to prevent climate change—even within developing countries—finds receptive listeners among women at every level in her own country.

"In traditional societies, women still do care for their families and their children," Ms. Mehra says. "India is no different. Women can see the impact of polluted air and water on their children and this is how the environmental message first reaches them."

A gender specialist by training, Malini Mehra has worked on sustainability, development and human rights issues for more than 20 years. For much of that time she has worked to convince the Government of India to shift from a policy of blame—criticizing developed countries for their historic role in causing climate change—to prevention—working to minimize the lead role her rapidly developing and demographically growing country (currently 1.2 billion people) could play in future greenhouse-gas emissions.

Leveraging such a shift is also the goal of her organization, the Centre for Social Markets, a non-governmental organization straddling bases in India

and the United Kingdom and dedicated to making markets work for what she calls the "triple bottom line": people, planet and profit. "Our goal is to reframe the debate from a victim-led 'can't-do-won't-do' mentality to a 'can-do-must-do' debate based on hope and good propositions," Ms. Mehra says.

In collaboration with an international network of partners and associates, the Centre for Social Markets leads many major public engagement initiatives, including Climate Challenge India to promote a proactive domestic response to climate change in India. This multi-year campaign strives to build a communication platform on climate change by using the media and focusing on city leadership, professional bodies and the business community. In a global competition hosted by the Consultative Group on International Agricultural Research, Climate Challenge India was selected as one of the world's top-five climate campaigns in 2007 and profiled at the United Nations' Climate Change Conference in Bali in December 2007.

The Centre for Social Markets is actively working to engage popular women's media in the country to help reach women in their homes and workplaces and mobilize them to act on climate change. "Women are a key constituency for us," Ms. Mehra says. "They are the real movers and shakers on

© Courtesy of Centre for Social Markets (CSM)

this issue in India. Through them we will make the change we are committed to."

Ms. Mehra says climate change will be felt differently by men and women—not because of inherent differences between the sexes—but because we continue to lead gendered lives, play different roles, and have different pressures and expectations. "In their roles as managers of the household economy, women—especially poor and marginalized women—will suffer from resource scarcity, disease and poor health, extreme weather events and displacement," she says. "We can anticipate the deprivations of the future because we can see them around us now. Hunger, malnutrition, conflict, these will all intensify as people's access to the basics in life—clean air, water, food and shelter—become compromised."

women-led organizations, are also beginning to appear in negotiating conferences.

Achieving greater representation of women in formal negotiations, as well as in the sectors of "global civil society" represented at climate meetings, is a critical first step toward gender equality in climate change work. Crucially, women must be involved not only in negotiations and planning but in implementation, which will involve a vast array of institutions. Given the complexity of human-climate interactions, a diversity of Government, intergovernmental and private entities will need to be engaged for decades in efforts to mitigate and adapt to climate change. Ensuring a gender perspective requires scrutiny of policy-making on energy, agriculture, health, disaster preparedness, and more. Women's voices will need to be forceful and heard, from tribal councils to national energy ministries to the halls of the United Nations.

Building mobilization capacity

It is not enough, however, simply to call for greater involvement of women. Governments sensitized by gender-aware publics and voters should remove obstacles to women's participation in the climate change debate. Gender equality will come closer to reality when Governments change laws and societies let go of the adverse norms and expectations that isolate women in the narrow confines of secondary citizenship and sexual and maternal roles defined by others. When societies expect legislative bodies to have at least 40 per cent women's participation, women are likely to step forward to fill the seats. But the other side of this coin is that life conditions—especially those relating to education, health and opportunity—must support women in reaching for and achieving personal and collective goals. It's worth asking what society can do, beyond the necessary task of changing laws and expectations, to make this transformation possible.

The concept of "human capital" may lend itself to a greater understanding about the roots of overall development, of gender equality and of the future of population growth. Wolfgang Lutz, leader of the World Population

The concept of "human capital" may lend itself to a greater understanding about the roots of overall development, of gender equality, and the future of population growth.

Program of the International Institute of Applied Systems Analysis in Austria, defines human capital as simply the combination of education and health in societies. "Human capital formation may even be the key for societies' adaptive capacity to climate change," Lutz suggests.[26]

Higher levels of educational attainment and their impact on reducing fertility are directly proportional to the number of years of schooling completed. Based on the experience of countries with more than 90 per cent of the world's population, according to the International Institute of Applied Systems Analysis, women who have never gone to school average 4.5 children each, while those who have completed a few years of primary school have just three. Women who complete one or two years of secondary school have an average of 1.9 children each, while those who complete one or two years of college have an average of just 1.7 children.[27] Lower fertility rates would contribute to slower population growth and in turn contribute to the reduction of future emissions and make it easier for Governments to keep pace with the need for adaptation to climate change.

As impressive as its impact on fertility, higher educational attainment—especially completion of several years of secondary school—also increases women's earnings, improves their life expectancy and the health outcomes of pregnancy and childbirth, and reduces infant mortality.[28] Each of these benefits is a mark of societies that are likely to be resilient in general, but specifically resilient to climate change. Moreover, going to school builds familiarity with wider circles of people and with cultural and social diversity, and it brings awareness of the world beyond one's doorstep. Women in many societies are still far more likely to spend most of their lives in and close to their homes. For them in particular, education facilitates the skills and confidence that can build capacity for mobilization for action, whether on climate change or other social concerns.

The other side of human capital—health—is at least as important as schooling to social resilience and mobilizing capacity. Societies can hardly be prosperous, dynamic and adaptive if mortality and morbidity rates are high. Health may be even more important to women's capacity to mobilize for change, since their reproductive roles and the expectations of their caregiving and other domestic responsibilities already force upon them high opportunity costs for outwardly directed social action.

Reproductive health is especially catalytic for women. From difficult pregnancies and childbirths to HIV and other sexually transmitted infections, reproductive health problems comprise the leading causes of death and disability among women worldwide.[29] Moreover, the lack of access to reproductive health services undermines achievement of most if not all of the Millennium Development Goals. That undoubtedly constitutes a further hindrance to social resilience and mobilization capacity.

---

31 **INDIA'S WOMEN FARMERS TACKLING CLIMATE CHANGE**

A collective of 5,000 women spread across 75 villages in the arid interior of Andhra Pradesh is now offering chemical-free, non-irrigated, organic agriculture as one method of combating global warming.

Agriculture accounts for 28 per cent of Indian greenhouse-gas emissions, mainly methane emission from paddy fields and cattle and nitrous oxides from fertilizers. A 2007 report by the Intergovernmental Panel on Climate Change says India's rainfall pattern will be changing disproportionately, with intense rain occurring over fewer days, leading directly to confusion in the agricultural scenario.

Decreased rain in December, January and February implies lesser storage and greater water stress, says the report, while more frequent and prolonged droughts are predicted. The report cites, as an example of impacts, that a rise in temperature of 0.5 degrees Celsius will reduce wheat production in India by 0.45 tons per hectare. Research at the School of Environmental Sciences in New Delhi projects crop losses of 10 per cent to 40 per cent by 2100 despite the beneficial effects of higher carbon dioxide on growth, with the dynamics of pests and diseases significantly altered.

In the village of Zaheerabad, *dalit* (the broken) women, forming the lowest rung of India's stratified society, now demonstrate adaptation to climate change by following a system of interspersing crops that do not need extra water, chemical inputs or pesticides for production.

The women grow as many as 19 types of indigenous crops to an acre, on arid, degraded lands that they have regenerated with help from an organization called the Deccan Development Society (DDS).

DDS, working in this area of India for the last 25 years, has helped these women acquire land through Government schemes for *dalits*, and form *sanghas* or local self-help groups that convene regularly and decide their own courses.

The women plant mostly in October-November, calling up the family's help for seven days for weeding and 15 to 20 days for harvesting. Farmyard manure is applied once in two or three years depending on soil conditions.

In Bidakanne village, 50-year-old Samamma, standing in her field, points out the various crops, all without water and chemical inputs, growing in between the rows of sunflowers: linseed, green pea, chickpea, various types of millet, wheat, safflower and legumes. The sunflower leaves attract pests and its soil depletion is compensated by the legumes which are nitrogen-fixing.

"In my type of cropping, one absorbs and one gives to the soil, while I get all my food requirements of oils, cereals and vegetable greens," says Samamma.

Samamma's under-one-acre plot produces, among other crops, 150 kilogrammes of red "horsegram," 200 kilogrammes of millet and 50 kilogrammes of linseed. She keeps 50 kilogrammes of grains and sells the rest in the open market.

The 5,000 women in 75 villages are now in various stages of adopting this method of agriculture.

"In the climate change framework, this system of dryland agriculture has the resilience to withstand all the fallouts of elevated temperatures," says P.V. Satheesh, the director of DDS.

The women now run a uniquely evolved system of "crop financing" and food-distribution that they have mapped out themselves. The money collected from open market sales every year is deposited in regular banks and the interest earned from them is used to finance loans for members who again complete the cycle by paying back their loan in grain over five years.

DDS has now involved the women in a monitored system of organic produce that is certified by the global Participatory Guarantee Scheme (PGS)'s Organic India Council. In Zaheerabad, the organically certified staples and grains are packed and labelled with the PGS certification, and taken by a mobile van to be sold retail to consumers in Hyderabad city. Satheesh says the women are swamped with orders.

By Keya Acharya. Excerpted with permission from Inter Press News Agency.

6 Five steps back from the brink

"Today we are faced with a challenge that calls for a shift in our thinking, so that humanity stops threatening its life-support system. We are called to assist the earth to heal her wounds and in the process heal our own—indeed, to embrace the whole creation in all its diversity, beauty and wonder."

—Wangari Maathai[1]

Global climate is changing. And it is we ourselves—in our lifestyles, our rapidly increasing numbers and the massive scale of our consumption and production—who are changing it.

Technology, especially the combustion of carbon-based fossil fuels that arose with the Industrial Revolution, has everything to do with this problem. Newer, cleaner technologies will be important to mitigating and adapting to climate change, but it is not technology that will save us. We will have to save ourselves. And to do this, we need to act on several fronts. Some of our actions will yield immediate benefits. Others only our children and grandchildren will appreciate. And yet we need to start all these actions at the same time. That time is now.

Climate change is often seen as a scientific issue, but its human dimensions are at last moving to the forefront. They will do so even more as the impacts of climate change unfold and societies respond to them. These impacts are likely to exacerbate gender and other social inequalities that are already acute today. Working now to reduce or eliminate such inequalities is thus a key anticipatory strategy for addressing climate change as well as contributing to development and the fullest exercise of human rights.

The complex nature and momentum of human-induced climate change suggest three areas of work needed now, with immediate, near term and long-term benefits.

Because it is already too late to *prevent* some amount of climate change, humanity must immediately learn to adapt to it and become more resilient to ongoing changes in the long run. Without halting the rise in global emissions of greenhouse gases and then rapidly reducing them, adaptation to climate change will become an endless—and maybe an impossible—challenge. The push to build our resilience to climate change cannot distract from the need to reduce emissions as rapidly as possible, starting now. But this requires a shift in human behaviour and a new mindset about the way we deal with our environment individually, collectively, locally, regionally and globally. Even the critically needed early successes in reducing emissions will be a prelude to a task likely to preoccupy humanity for decades, even centuries: prospering globally while keeping human activities from sending the global atmosphere and climate outside the range of human habitability.

In considering how such an ambitious task might be undertaken, there can be no escaping a difference among countries identified in the United Nations Framework Convention on Climate Change (UNFCCC) itself. As a group, developed countries have contributed a much greater load of greenhouse-gas emissions to the atmosphere—and hence to the currently elevated concentrations of these heat-trapping gases in the atmosphere—than developing countries. This is especially evident when these emissions are calculated as per capita emissions based on these countries' past and present populations. For the most part the industrialized countries also have a greater economic and institutional capacity than developing ones to respond to climate change and its impacts. And this greater capacity stems in part from the fact that in emitting greenhouse gases over many decades they have developed economically. Their per capita incomes are high by global standards. If developed countries decline to make early and proportionally greater efforts to address climate change, it is very difficult to see which other countries could take the lead.

The world needs innovative ideas on how to bring both high-emitting and low-emitting countries to an agreement that can reduce emissions and provide the financing and technology needed to enable all countries and all people to adapt and build resilience to climate change. A group of authors at Princeton University in the United States recently suggested that countries' obligations to reduce emissions should be based on the share of the world's 1 billion wealthiest people living within their borders. Since low-income countries too are home to wealthy individuals—who are also high emitters of greenhouse gases—a formula based on each population of these individuals might have some potential to break the impasse between developed and developing countries over responsibility and capacity to address climate change.[2] Whether this specific idea (based in part on a long-standing concept known as greenhouse development rights) moves forward or not, a global conversation is increasingly needed to generate workable ideas to address climate-change mitigation and adaptation on the basis of equity and human rights.

Societies' adaptation and resilience to climate change can benefit from greater gender equality and access to reproductive health care. Both facilitate women's full participation in their communities' and societies' development and climate change resilience. And both encourage positive democratic trends that arise from women exercising choice over childbearing that also yields benefits in poverty alleviation and the management of natural resources and the environment.

Immediate mitigation—rapid reductions in emissions—is a complex and politically sensitive challenge. It is the major topic before the negotiators in Copenhagen in December 2009. It is possible that population growth

in developed countries, and conceivably in some large and rapidly developing ones, will arise as among the factors to be considered in setting goals for emissions reductions. The long-term effort to maintain population-wide human well-being in balance with atmosphere and climate will ultimately require sustainable patterns of consumption and production that can only be achieved and maintained in the context of a sustainable world population. Over decades and centuries the trajectory that world population follows will help determine the levels of per capita emissions of greenhouse gases that will be consistent with a stable atmosphere and climate.

Since the 1994 International Conference on Population and Development (ICPD), however, the world has learned that trying to "control" human population risks depriving women of their right to determine how many children to have and when to have them. What we can work toward instead is environmentally sustainable population dynamics that are characterized by safe childbearing, long life expectancies and freedom for individuals to make their own reproductive health decisions. We can also step up our efforts to support young people so they may live productive lives and fully realize their rights to education and health.

Five steps suggest themselves for action as negotiators gather in Copenhagen in December 2009, and may therefore help humanity retreat from the brink.

1: Bring a better understanding of population dynamics, gender and reproductive health to climate change and environmental discussions at all levels

A lack of awareness of the rights-based population policy agenda forged at the ICPD continues to plague climate negotiators' discussions. The Intergovernmental Panel on Climate Change's 2007 report on mitigation, for example, suggested that the international community would have to restrict its policy options for limiting future emissions to those leading to reductions in energy use and carbon intensities, rather than any that might help slow population growth, because the "scope and legitimacy of population control" was still "subject to ongoing debate."[3]

Since the ICPD, the international community was thought to have abandoned misguided discussions about

© Doug Murray/Reuters/Corbis

the "scope and legitimacy of population control." Control of population, in the sense of Government edicts and targets on fertility levels, has no ethical place in contemporary rights-based policymaking. What is ethical—and in the long run far more effective than governmental controls—are policies that enable women and their partners to decide for themselves if and when to have children and to do so in good health, and actions that promote equality between the sexes in all aspects of economic and social life.

Demographic research has demonstrated for decades that when women and their partners can take advantage of client-focused family planning services, fertility falls. Particularly when combined with education for girls and economic opportunities for women, family planning services and supplies are especially powerful in delaying the age of first pregnancies and reducing the size of completed families.[4] Even in the absence of strong initiatives in other areas, family planning almost universally proves popular, and its availability quickly influences childbearing patterns. As Governments have expanded health services that allow women and their partners to plan their families, contraceptive prevalence has become the norm in developing as well as developed countries, and family size has fallen by 50 per cent. Today, the global total fertility

rate stands at 2.5 children—not far above the replacement fertility rate of 2.1 children that would prevail worldwide if there were no significant infant and child mortality.[5]

Outmoded attitudes about "population control" have been replaced by more holistic, rights- and health-based views about population dynamics and their relationship to climate change. In December 2008, the Asian Forum of Parliamentarians for Population and Development stated, "There are strong linkages and correlation between population growth and emission of greenhouse gases that cause climate change, and … communities experiencing high population growth are also most vulnerable to the negative effects of climate change, such as water scarcity, failed crops, rise in sea level, and the spread of infectious diseases." The parliamentarians—representing 20 countries—called for efforts to "support and empower poor and marginalized people" in combating climate change, and the integration of "gender perspectives into climate policymaking to ensure outcomes benefit both women and men equally and equitably."[6]

Research has shown for more than 15 years that merely satisfying unmet demand for family planning services would enable developing countries to meet their targets for lower fertility rates.[7] And every nation that offers

▲ A family receives family planning advice at Kivunge Hospital, Zanzibar.
© Sala Lewis/UNFPA

women a full range of options for their own management of the timing of childbearing has fertility rates that are at replacement level or lower.[8] These low rates are not restricted to developed countries. They also characterize developing countries—including Iran, Thailand, Tunisia, Cuba and Mauritius—in which reproductive health care and contraceptive choices are readily available. The route to a climate-sustainable human population therefore lies in the removal of barriers to the use of family planning and the rights-based population policies envisioned by conferees in Cairo in 1994.

2: Fully fund family planning services and contraceptive supplies within the framework of reproductive health and rights, and assure that low income is no barrier to access

One of the achievements of the ICPD Programme of Action was the elaboration of the holistic concept of reproductive health. This term embraces the full spectrum of sexual and reproductive well-being and autonomy of women, men and young people. A positive outcome of

this elaboration was a significant increase in international spending on aspects of reproductive health beyond the family planning activities that had long been the foundation of population policies and programmes. Starting in 1986, global spending on prevention and treatment of HIV and AIDS was about $1 billion annually until the start of the new millennium, when the amount began rising rapidly and is now about $10 billion.[9]

That amount is less than the need, but as HIV and AIDS and other health issues have preoccupied Governments, and as fertility rates have generally continued their long-term decline from peaks in the middle of the 20th century, spending on family planning has fallen significantly. In the meantime, declines in fertility noted in most developing countries over the past few decades have stalled in some countries at levels well above replacement levels, and fertility has actually risen in some developed countries, such as the United States. The United Nations Population Division's projections on which development experts and climate scientists now rely suggest that there will be between 8 billion and 10.5 billion people by 2050. Even the Population Division's low-growth scenario is based on the assumption of continuing declines of fertility.[10] "No official projection considers the alarming implications if global contraceptive use declines—as it could without greater investment in family planning programmes," note five former directors of the population and reproductive health programme of the United States Agency for International Development."[11]

Research and experience suggest that individual interest in family planning may be heightened by the impacts of climate change, as natural resource scarcity and economic stress have done in the past. In South Africa, for example, hard economic times and the depletion of farmland encouraged more women to take up contraception from the 1970s through the early 1990s. "Black women assumed management of their fertility because they found themselves in precarious circumstances," explained Population Council researcher Carol Kaufman, who studied the history of South African contraceptive use in this period. "The fear and economic desperation stirred by the thought of another child should not be underestimated."[12]

Other examples around the world demonstrate that women who have access to the right resources and equal opportunities are even more likely to choose family planning and have later and safer pregnancies and the smaller families that it facilitates. Each year of completed schooling contributes as well, as do increases in child survival that offer parents confidence their children will outlive them. The key point is that women and men themselves, not Governments or any other institutions, make the decisions on childbearing that contribute to an environmentally sustainable human population. "Even in the poorest part of the Third World," Nobel laureate economist Amartya Sen wrote of the combination of empowered women, family planning access and low fertility rates in Kerala, India, "the solution to the population problem may be reconciled with reproductive freedom."[13]

3: Prioritize research and data collection to improve the understanding of gender and population dynamics in climate change mitigation and adaptation

Although population data are generally regarded as among the success stories of social science, their integration with the developing science of climate change and its human dimen-

---

32 FUNDING FOR FAMILY PLANNING FALLS

Overall spending by donor countries for all population-related activities (those laid out in the ICPD Programme of Action) in developing countries has been rising steadily in recent years, reaching $7.4 billion in 2006 and estimated to have surpassed $8 billion in 2007. But as noted in Chapter 5, donor assistance for one of those activities—provision of family planning services—fell from $723 million in 1995 to $338 million in 2007. That decline means that funding for family planning, as a share of total funding for all population-related activities, fell from about 55 per cent in 1995 to about 5 per cent in 2007.[14] Yet, unmet need for these services remains high.[15] Unmet need correlates strongly with poverty, with the poorest women and couples least likely to have access to family planning services and least likely to be using contraception despite the intention to avoid pregnancy.[16] Since the development of the Programme of Action, most growth in spending on family planning has occurred in a handful of large developing countries, while spending in most developing countries has been relatively stable at low levels.[17]

Low levels of funding for family planning undermine efforts to achieve the Millennium Development Goals, including those related to gender equality, education, and environmental sustainability. While climate change mitigation and adaptation are not among these goals, efforts at the community and global levels to address climate change and its impacts will meet greater challenges in the face of the high fertility that results from poor access to voluntary family planning. In the words of Thoraya Ahmed Obaid, Executive Director of UNFPA, "There is no investment in development that costs so little and brings benefits that are so far-reaching and enormous."[18]

---

sions remains poor. This applies not only to the influence of population growth on greenhouse-gas emissions and climate change adaptation, but also to the interactions with climate change of such other population dynamics as migration, urbanization and changing age structures.

More work is also required to understand the interactions between gender and climate change. Few data sets related to natural disasters or other potential climate change impacts have been disaggregated by sex. Quantifications of differential gender impacts are common in the literature on disasters, but the original authoritative sources of commonly cited facts and figures are typically elusive. Similarly, common assessments of

▲ *A woman boils water in kettles heated by solar energy panels in Pengyang County, China.*
© Reuters

women's representation in occupations, their ownership of land, or their use of natural resources are often based on a single estimate or extrapolated from a handful of local case studies. Although half the world's population now lives in cities or other urban areas, climate-relevant research on women and population has focused mostly on the rural experience. Research can be improved through greater participation of women and marginalized groups themselves. This idea, developed by women participating in a conference on climate change and gender in Dakar in 2008, could shed light on differences between consumption generated by males and females, paving the way for a better understanding of gender connections to climate change mitigation.[19] Mapping gender, population and climate change can vary in its technological sophistication from the use of Geographic Information Systems software to rapid appraisals based on the knowledge and experience of members of neighbourhoods and communities. Climate-related proposals of all kinds, from community initiatives to the work of the UNFCCC, can benefit from "gender-impact assessments" that consider differential effects on women and men. Budgets and spending in climate funds administered by the World Bank and others should be scrutinized through a gender lens.

Some of this is an issue of greater resource investment, but much of it is a matter of political will and a greater sensitivity to the importance of population and gender by researchers, data collectors and programme developers.

In 2010, many countries will carry out censuses, which will present an opportunity to gather data about individuals and households that may help shape policies to mitigate greenhouse-gas emissions and aid adaptation to the effects of climate change. Ideally, climate-change specialists would be involved in the design of national censuses. The outputs of these censuses could then inform future projections of greenhouse-gas emissions and climate-change impacts, as well as policymaking and planning for mitigation and adaptation.

4: Improve the sex-disaggregation of data related to migration flows that are influenced by environmental factors and prepare now for increases in population movements resulting from climate change

The environmental factors that induce people to look for new homes may be related to causes other than climate change and may be only part of the cause of any particular movement of people. Much more research is needed on the reasons for migration, which will differ from place to place according to specifics of culture and circumstance.

Awareness-raising and proactive intervention require better understanding of the links between the movement of people and various environmental factors. There is a need for innovative research methods and multidisciplinary approaches to generate credible quantitative estimates and forecasts of the affected populations and to identify "hotspot" countries for targeted assistance. Multi-stakeholder involvement in the research process is essential. It is equally important to enhance the data collection capacities of those countries most likely to be affected by environmental migration. This can ensure they have an adequate research base in order to inform policy and programmes.

Since women and men may move for different reasons and face different situations in migration— different livelihoods, resources, opportunities and vulnerabilities— gender considerations are paramount in formulating polices related to migration.

On the operational side, it is also important to build the capacity of Governments and other relevant stakeholders to respond to the challenges presented by the intersection of climate change, environment and migration. Addressing such challenges requires a holistic operational approach that covers all types of environmentally induced population movements. Strengthening the humanitarian response in order to provide effective assistance and protection to populations displaced by a disaster is the first step.

Humanitarian and development institutions need to be sensitive to the human-rights challenges that displacement creates. Climate change is projected to affect the most vulnerable in society: female-headed households, children, marginalized minorities, indigenous peoples, the disabled, the ill, the elderly and the poor. In displacement scenarios, this vulnerability will take the form of unequal access to food, water, shelter, medical attention, educa-

Those countries with largest historical responsibility for loading the atmosphere with heat-trapping gases also bear the largest obligation to help, and indeed accommodate, those made destitute by the consequences of global atmospheric change for which they themselves bear little responsibility.

tion, transportation and other basic necessities. When designing programmes to respond to the humanitarian and social impacts of climate change, it is essential to devise strategies that are gender sensitive and uphold the human rights of those affected. Migration and resettlement policies should take gender into account so they have a positive impact on both women and men.

It is also important to look beyond humanitarian relief and move toward more proactive measures, increasing efforts to integrate disaster-risk reduction, including preparedness, early warning and prevention, into operational activities in disaster-prone areas. Following the emergency phase, efforts should also be made to ensure effective recovery. Actors on the ground should rapidly turn their efforts to finding durable solutions for displaced populations and possibly facilitating their voluntary return. Community-stabilization programmes can be used to support this objective and to link recovery efforts with sustainable development by providing affected families an opportunity to engage in productive activities. Ensuring better management and planning for environmentally induced population flows is also needed. This may include factoring such movements into urban planning.

In negotiating responsibilities and capacities relating to the UNFCCC, Governments should consider establishing obligations to address the migration or forced displacement of peoples resulting from sea-level rise or other environmental conditions that can be clearly linked to climate change. Those countries with largest historical responsibility for loading the atmosphere with heat-trapping gases also bear the largest obligation to help, and indeed accommodate, those made destitute by the consequences of global atmospheric change for which they themselves bear little responsibility. Where return to degraded areas is possible, circular migration that contributes to the development of sending countries can be integrated into adaptation efforts financed by new funding mechanisms that emerge for this purpose. Migration itself should be seen as a mechanism for adaptation, and the capacity to migrate and to accommodate and integrate migrants should be recognized as an important aspect of climate change resilience.

All the above will only be possible with regional, international, and global collaboration and coordination reaching not only across countries, but also across disciplines, incorporating climate science, geography, migration, development studies and health. Also critical will be collaboration involving Governments, international organizations, civil society, local communities and the private sector.

Censuses to be carried out by many countries in 2010 should gather information that may result in insights into the extent to which people have already migrated in response to environmental or climate change and that may result in better projections of population movements. Equipped with complete and accurate information, policymakers, Governments and international organizations may then help anticipate migration as a part of adaptation to climate change.

5: Integrate gender considerations into global efforts to mitigate and adapt to climate change

The mandates of Governments and other institutions to consider women's circumstances and gender relations have been established in declarations of rights and other agreements predating the world's current focus on climate change.[20] The Programme of Action placed sexual and reproductive health at the centre of women's equality with men and their dignity and capacities as human beings. The Platform of Action agreed to at the Fourth World Conference on Women in Beijing in 1995 called for gender mainstreaming in development and human affairs generally, meaning a fundamental consideration of differential impacts of policies and programmes on women and men as the rule rather than the exception. The Convention on the Elimination of All Forms of Discrimination against Women, which went into force in 1981, commits ratifying nations to conform their legislation and legal system with gender equality and to eliminate all distinctions, exclusions or restrictions made on the basis of sex.

The Copenhagen climate change summit in 2009 and the processes that will follow it offer opportunities to bring gender considerations to this critical global discussion. The integration of gender should begin with the participation of women, men and gender experts in national delegations and in the negotiations themselves. Gender considerations should also be mainstreamed into climate-related research on livelihoods, resources use, vulnerability and impact. Natural disasters, likely to increase as the global climate changes, point to a compelling and urgent need to understand how gender affects people's responses to crises. The time to do that, however, is well before disaster strikes. The concept of disaster-risk reduction is based on the recognition that disasters will occur but that informed and committed societies can anticipate them and their effects and thereby minimize loss of life and property and accelerate recovery efforts. In this work it is critical to consider the kinds of gender differences that make women disproportionately vulnerable in disasters and that sometimes discriminates against them in the recovery process. Women and their children must be visible to responders to ensure the success of post-disaster recovery and have a say in the formulation of disaster risk-reduction plans.

None of these are steps to be taken in isolation from broader social efforts to achieve gender equality. Action is critically needed to increase women's ownership of land and legal control of the critical natural resources on which many of their lives depend. Assuring equal protection of the law, opportunities to engage in the formal economic sector, and access to reproductive health not only build gender equality but contribute to societies' resilience in the face of all kinds of rapid change, of which climate change is perhaps the most hazardous.

There is still time for the negotiators about to gather in Copenhagen to think creatively about population, reproductive health and gender equality, and how these may contribute to a just and environmentally sustainable world. These linkages may indeed offer an arena where the universal exercise of human rights would help us resolve what today seems an almost insoluble challenge: managing human-induced climate change and improving human lives and livelihoods even as it occurs.[21]

Notes and indicators

Notes

OVERVIEW

1 Ban, K. 2007. "A New Green Economics." *The Washington Post*, 3 December, p. A17.

2 United Nations Environment Programme. 2009. *UNEP Yearbook 2009*. Nairobi: United Nations Environment Programme.

3 World Bank. 2008. *Development and Climate Change: A Strategic Framework for the World Bank Group.* Washington, D.C.: World Bank.

4 Asian Development Bank. 2009. *The Economics of Climate Change in Southeast Asia: A Regional Review.* Manila: Asian Development Bank.

5 Ibid.

6 Costello, A. and others. 2009. "Managing the Health Effects of Climate Change." *The Lancet* 373 (9676): 1693-1733.

7 Aguilar, L., M. Blanco and I. Dankelman. 2006. "The Absence of Gender Equity in the Discussions on the International Regime on Access and Benefit Sharing." Discussion document for the Eighth Meeting of the Conference of the Parties to the Convention on Biological Diversity. Gland: International Union for Conservation and Nature.

8 World Health Organization. 2009. *Reproductive Health.* Geneva: website: http://www.who.int/topics/reproductive_health/en/, accessed 23 July 2009.

9 Patz, J. A. and others. 2005. "Impact of Regional Climate Change on Human Health." *Nature* 438: 310-317.

10 World Health Organization. 2005. "Climate and Health Fact Sheet." July. Geneva: World Health Organization. Website: http://www.who.int/globalchange/news/fsclimandhealth/en/index.html, accessed 24 July 2009.

11 United Nations Department of Economic and Social Affairs. 1999. The World at Six Billion (Document ESA/P/WP.154). 12 October 1999. New York: United Nations. Website: http://www.un.org/esa/population/publications/sixbillion/sixbilpart1.pdf, accessed 28 July 2009. United Nations Department of Economic and Social Affairs, Population Division. 2009. *World Population Prospects:*

The 2008 Revision. New York: United Nations. Website: http://esa.un.org/unpp, accessed 28 July 2009.

12 Bongaarts, J., B.C. O'Neill and S.R. Gaffin. 1997. "Global Warming Policy: Population Left Out in the Cold." *Environment* 39 (9): 40-41.

13 Jiang, L. and K. Hardee. 2009. "How Do Recent Population Trends Matter to Climate Change?" Working Paper. Washington, D.C.: Population Action International.

14 UNFPA and the International Institute for Environment and Development, in collaboration with the Population Division of the United Nations and UN-HABITAT, brought together 40 demographers, scientists, and experts in population, gender and development in London in June 2009 to share the latest thinking and research on mitigating climate change through reductions in greenhouse-gas emissions and on adapting to the effects of current and future climate change. For a complete list of conclusions from the event, visit the UNFPA website at www.unfpa.org/public/News/events/ccpd.

15 Oldrup, H. and M. H. Breengaard. 2009. "Gender and Climate Changes Report." Nordic Summit Declaration, Abstract—Desk Study on Gender Equality and Climate Changes. Nordic Council of Ministers. Website: http://www.norden.org/gender/doks/sk/Gender_and_climate_changes_Rapport.pdf, accessed 12 April 2009.

16 United Nations Development Programme. 2009. "Resource Guide on Gender and Climate Change." New York: United Nations Development Programme.

17 Parry, M.L. and others. 2007. "Summary for Policymakers." *Climate Change 2007: Impacts, Adaptation and Vulnerability. Contribution of Working Group II to the Fourth Assessment Report of the Intergovernmental Panel on Climate Change.* Cambridge: Cambridge University Press.

18 United Nations Framework Convention on Climate Change. 2009. Website: http://unfccc.int/essential_background/convention/

background/items/1349.php, accessed 23 July 2009.

19 Mutunga, C. and K. Hardee. 2009. "Population and Reproductive Health in National Adaptation Programmes of Action (NAPAs) for Climate Change" (draft). Washington, D.C.: Population Action International.

20 International Conference on Population and Development. 1994. *Programme of Action,* paragraphs 1.2 and 10.7. Website: http://www.unfpa.org/icpd/icpd-programme.cfm, accessed 23 July 2009.

CHAPTER 1

1 This chapter has been adapted from the United Nations Environment Programme's *UNEP Yearbook 2009* but draws on other sources, such as the Worldwatch Institute.

2 Gillet, N.P. and others. 2008. "Attribution of Polar Warming to Human Influence." *Nature Geoscience* (1): 750-754.

3 Kay, J., T. I'Ecuyer, A. Gettelman, G. Stephens and C. O'Dell. 2008. "The Contribution of Cloud and Radiation Anomalies to the 2007 Arctic Sea Ice Extent Minimum." *Geophysical Research Letter,* 35, L08503, doi:10.1029/2008GL033451; National Snow and Ice Data Center. 2008. "Arctic Sea Ice News and Analysis." Website: http://nsidc.org/arcticseaice-news/, accessed 23 July 2009.

4 McKeown, A. and G. Gardner. 2009. *Climate Change Reference Guide.* Washington, D.C.: Worldwatch Institute.

5 Perovich, D.K., J.A. Richter-Menge, K.F. Jones and B. Light. 2008. "Sunlight, Water and Ice: Extreme Arctic Sea Ice Melt During the Summer of 2007. *Geophysical Research Letter,* 35, L11501, doi:10.1029/2008GL034007.

6 Kay, J., T. I'Ecuyer, A. Gettelman, G. Stephens and C. O'Dell. 2008. "The Contribution of Cloud and Radiation Anomalies to the 2007 Arctic Sea Ice Extent Minimum. *Geophysical Research Letter,* 35, L08503, doi:10.1029/2008GL033451.

7 Holland, D.M. and others. 2008. "Acceleration of Jakobshavn

Isbrae Triggered by Warm Subsurface Ocean Waters." *Nature Geoscience* 1(10): 659-664.

8 Charbit, S., D. Paillard and G. Ramstein. 2008. "Amount of Carbon Dioxide Emissions Irreversibly Leading to the Total of Melting of Greenland." *Geophysical Research Letter,* 35, L12503, doi:10.1029/2008GL033472.

9 Rignot, E. and others. 2008. "Recent Antarctic Ice Mass Loss from Radar Interferometry and Regional Climate Modelling." *Nature Geoscience* 1(2): 106-110.

10 Dahl-Jensen, D. 2009. "Greenland Ice Sheet in a Changing Climate," cited in *Climate Change: Global Risks, Challenges and Decisions.* Copenhagen, University of Copenhagen, 10-12 March, p. 9.

11 Pfeffer, W.T., J.T. Harper and S. O'Neel. 2008. "Kinematic Constraints on Glacier Contributions to 21st Century Sea-level Rise." *Science* 321(5894): 1340-1343.

12 Jevrejeva, S. and others. 2008. "Recent Global Sea Level Acceleration Started over 200 Years Ago?" *Geophysical Research Letter,* 35, L08715, doi:10.1029/2008GL033611.

13 Carlson, A.E. and others. 2008. "Rapid Early Holocene Deglaciation of the Laurentide Ice Sheet." *Nature Geoscience,* 1 (9): 620-624.

14 UN-HABITAT. 2008. *State of the World's Cities 2008/9: Harmonious Cities.* London: Earthscan.

15 Semiletov, I. 2008. *International Siberian Shelf Study 2008.* International Arctic Research Center, ISS08-Update, 15 September 2008. Website: http://www.iarc.uaf.edu/expeditions/?cat=8, accessed 23 July 2009; Shaw, J. 2002. "The Meltwater Hypothesis for Subglacial Bedforms." *Quaternary International* 90 (2002): 5-22.

16 Khvorostyanov, D.V. and others. 2008. "Vulnerability of East Siberia's Frozen Carbon Stores to Future Warming." *Geophysical Research Letter,* 35, L10703, doi:10.1029/2008GL033639.

17 Ise, T. and others. 2008. "High Sensitivity of Peat Decomposition to Climate Change through

Water-Table Feedback." *Nature Geoscience,* doi: 10.1038/ngeo331.

18   Global Carbon Project 2008. "Carbon Budget and Trends 2007." Website: www.globalcarbon-project.org; Canadell, J.G. and M.R. Raupach. 2008. "Managing Forest for Climate Change Mitigation." *Science* 320 (5882): 1456-1457.

19   Piao, S. and others. 2008. "Net Carbon Dioxide Losses of Northern Ecosystems in Response to Autumn Warming." *Nature* 451 (7174): 49-53.

20   Ramanathan, V. and G. Carmichael. 2008. "Global and Regional Climate Changes Due to Black Carbon." *Nature Geoscience* 1(4): 221-226.

21   Ibid.

22   Elsner, J.B., J.P. Kossin and T.H. Jagger. 2008. "The Increasing Intensity of the Strongest Tropical Cyclones." *Nature* 455 (7209): 92-94.

23   Barnett, T.P. and D.W. Pierce. 2008. "When Will Lake Mead Go Dry?" *Water Resources Research* 44, W03201, doi:10.1029/2007WR006704.

24   All items in box from the International Union for Conservation and Nature, the United Nations Development Programme, the Stockholm International Water Institute, the Organization for Economic Cooperation and Development or the United Nations.

CHAPTER 2

1   Bernstein, L. and others. 2007. *Climate Change 2007: Synthesis Report. Fourth Assessment Report of the Intergovernmental Panel on Climate Change,* Table 5.1, p. 67. Website: http://www.ipcc.ch/index.htm, accessed 23 July 2009; For 2-degree threshold, see Watkins, K. and others. 2007. "Fighting Climate Change: Human Solidarity in a Divided World," *Human Development Report 2007/2008.* New York: United Nations Development Programme. Website: http://hdr.undp.org/en/reports/global/hdr2007-2008/, accessed 23 July 2009.

2   Hare, W.L. 2008. "A Safe Landing for Climate," in Engelman, R., M. Renner and J. Sawin, eds., *State of*

the World 2009: Into a Warming World.* New York: Norton; Lynas, M. 2009. "Preventing Dangerous Climate Change," in *Six Degrees: Our Future on a Hotter Planet.* Washington, D.C.: National Geographic.

3   Smith, P. (author), and M. Bertaglia (editor). 2007. "Greenhouse Gas Mitigation in Agriculture." *Encyclopedia of Earth.* Cleveland,: C. J., editor. Washington, D.C.: Environmental Information Coalition, National Council for Science and the Environment. Website: http://www.eoearth.org/article/Greenhouse_gas_mitigation_in_agriculture, accessed 23 July 2009.

4   British Petroleum. 2008. *Statistical Review of World Energy.* London: British Petroleum; Marland, G. and others. 2007. "Global, Regional, and National Fossil Fuel CO_2 Emissions," *Trends: A Compendium of Data on Global Change.* Oak Ridge: Carbon Dioxide International Analysis Center, Oak Ridge National Laboratory, U.S. Department of Energy.

5   International Energy Agency. 2008. *International Energy Outlook 2008.* Paris: International Energy Agency.

6   Carbon Dioxide International Analysis Center. 2009. *National CO_2 Emissions from Fossil-Fuel Burning, Cement Manufacture, and Gas Flaring: 1751-2006.* Oak Ridge: Carbon Dioxide International Analysis Center, Oak Ridge National Laboratory, U.S. Department of Energy.

7   Ibid.

8   Hansen, J. and others. 2008. "Target Atmospheric CO2: Where Should Humanity Aim?" New York: Columbia University. Website: http://www.columbia.edu/~jeh1/2008/TargetCO2_20080407.pdf, accessed 2 July 2009; Meinshausen, M. and others. 2009. "Greenhouse-gas Emission Targets for Limiting Global Warming to 2C." *Nature* 458 (7242): 1158.

9   Rogner, H.-H. and others. 2007. "Introduction." *Climate Change 2007: Mitigation, Contribution of Working Group III to the Fourth Assessment Report of the*

Intergovernmental Panel on Climate Change. Cambridge: Cambridge University Press.

10   International Energy Agency. 2006. *World Energy Outlook 2006.* Paris: International Energy Agency.

11   World Resources Institute. 2009. *Summary of UNFCCC Submissions* (Working Paper, June). Website: http://pdf.wri.org/working_papers/unfccc_wri_submissions.pdf, accessed 21 July 2009.

12   Rahman, A., N. Robins and A. Roncerel. 1993. *Consumption versus Population: Which Is the Climate Bomb? Exploding the Population Myth.* Brussels: Climate Network Europe.

13   Pearce, F. 2009. "Consumption Dwarfs Population as Main Environmental Threat." Yale Environment 360/Guardian Environmental Network. Website: http://www.guardian.co.uk/environment/2009/apr/15/consumption-versus-population-environmental-impact, accessed 20 April 2009.

14   Holdren, J. P. 1991. "Population and the Energy Problem." *Population and Environment* 12 (3): 231-255.

15   Eilperin, J. and S. Mufson. 2009. "Renewable Energy's Environmental Paradox." *The Washington Post.* 16 April, p. A1.

16   Sedgh, G. and others. 2007. "Induced Abortion: Rates and Trends Worldwide." *The Lancet,* 370 (9595): 1338-1345; Alan Guttmacher Institute. 1999. *Sharing Responsibility: Women, Society and Abortion Worldwide.* New York: Alan Guttmacher Institute; United Nations Department of Economic and Social Affairs, Population Division. 2005. *World Population Prospects: The 2004 Revision.* New York: United Nations; Leridon, H. 1977. *Human Fertility: The Basic Components.* Chicago: University of Chicago Press, 1977. All cited in Guttmacher Institute. 2007. "Abortion: Worldwide Levels and Trends" (PowerPoint presentation).

17   Alan Guttmacher Institute. October 2007. New York. "Abortion: Worldwide Levels and Trends."(PowerPoint presentation). Website: http://www.guttmacher.org/presentations/

AWWtrends.html, accessed 9 July 2009.

18   United Nations Department of Economic and Social Affairs, Population Division. 2009: *World Population Prospects: The 2008 Revision.* New York: United Nations.

19   United Nations Economic and Social Council. 2009. "World Population Monitoring, Focusing on the Contribution of the Programme of Action of the International Conference on Population and Development to the Internationally Agreed Development Goals, Including the Millennium Development Goals." Document E/CN.9/2009/3. Website: http://daccessdds.un.org/doc/UNDOC/GEN/N09/212/29/PDF/N0921229.pdf?OpenElement, accessed 21 April 2009.

20   Ibid.

21   MacKellar, F. L. and others. 1995. "Population, Number of Households, and Global Warming." *Popnet* (27): 1-3.

22   Cole, M.A. and E. Neumayer. 2004. "Examining the Impact of Demographic Factors on Air Pollution." *Population and Environment* 26 (1): 5-21.

23   Dalton, M. and others. 2008. "Population Aging and Future Carbon Emissions in the United States." *Energy Economics* 30 (2008): 642-675. Website: http://www.iiasa.ac.at/Research/PCC/pubs/Dalton_etal_EE2008.pdf, accessed 22 April 2009; Dalton, M., L. Jiang, S. Pachauri and B. C. O'Neill. 2008. "Demographic Change and Future Carbon Emissions in China and India." Paper presented at the Annual Meeting of the Population Association of America, 28-31 March 2007, New York. Revised 2008. Website: http://www.iiasa.ac.at/Research/PCC/pubs/dem-emiss/Daltonetal_PAA2007.pdf, accessed 22 April 2009.

24   Satterthwaite, D. and D. Dodman. 2009. "The Role of Cities in Climate Change," in *State of the World 2009: Into a Warming World.* (Engelman, R., M. Renner and J. Sawin, eds.) New York: Norton.

25   Ibid.

26 Organization for Economic Cooperation and Development. 2008. "Promoting Sustainable Consumption: Good Practices in OECD Countries" and "Environmental Policy and Household Behaviour: Evidence in the Areas of Energy, Food, Transport, Waste and Water." Paris: Organization for Economic Cooperation and Development.

27 Caiazzo, A. and A. Barrett. 2003. "Engaging Women in Environmental Activism: Recommendations for Rachel's Network." Washington, D.C.: Institute for Women's Policy Research. Website: http://www.iwpr.org/pdf/I913.pdf, accessed 9 April 2009; Bord, R. and R. O'Connor. 1997. "The Gender Gap in Environmental Attitudes: The Case of Perceived Vulnerability to Risk." *Social Science Quarterly* 78 (December):830-40; Brunette, D. 2008. "NPD Reports Women Are More Keen on 'Green'" (press release). Port Washington: The NPD Group.

28 European Commission and the European Parliament. 2008. *Europeans' Attitudes Towards Climate Change.* Website: http://ec.europa.eu/public_opinion/archives/ebs/ebs_300_full_en.pdf, accessed 23 July 2009; Central Office of Information 2005. "Attitudes to Climate Change—Wave 1: Top Line Summary." London: Department of Environment, Food and Rural Affairs (UK). Website: http://www.defra.gov.uk/ENVIRONMENT/climatechange/uk/individual/attitudes/pdf/ccresearch-toplines1-0503.pdf, accessed 23 July 2009; Hunter, L., A. Hatch and A. Johnson. 2004. "Cross-National Gender Variation in Environmental Behaviors." Boulder: University of Colorado.

29 Davies, K. 2008. "Alive: Culture, Sustainability and Intergenerational Democracy." *UNESCO E-journal.* Edition 2. ISSN: 1835 – 2776. Website: http://www.abp.unimelb.edu.au/unesco/ejournal/pdf/kirsten-davies.pdf, accessed 23 July 2009.

30 Johnsson-Latham, G. 2007. *A Study on Gender Equality as a Prerequisite for Sustainable Development.* Report to the Environment Advisory Council, Sweden. Stockholm: Ministry of the Environment (Sweden).

31 O'Neill, B.C. 2009 (in press: tentative publication date October 2009). "Climate Change and Population Growth," in Mazur, L. 2009. *A Pivotal Moment: Population, Justice and the Environmental Challenge.* Island Press, Washington, D.C.; Pacala, S. and R. Socolow. 2007. "Stabilization Wedges: Solving the Climate Problem for the Next 50 Years with Current Technologies." Science 305: 968-972.

32 Pacala, S. and R. Socolow. 2007. "Stabilization Wedges: Solving the Climate Problem for the Next 50 Years with Current Technologies." *Science* 305: 968-972.

33 Jowitt, J. and P. Wintour. 2008. "Cost of Tackling Climate Change Has Doubled, Warns Stern." *The Guardian* 26 June.

34 United Nations Department of Economic and Social Affairs, Population Division. 2009. Website: http://esa.un.org/unpp/index.asp, accessed 23 July 2009.

35 Wheeler, D. and D. Hammer. (Forthcoming in 2009.) "The Economics of Population Policy for Carbon Emissions Reduction." Working Paper. Washington, D.C.: Center for Global Development.

36 Panel on Policy Implications of Greenhouse Warming. 1992. *Policy Implications of Greenhouse Warming: Mitigation, Adaptation, and the Science Base.* Washington, D.C.: National Academies Press, p. 811. Website: http://books.nap.edu/openbook.php?record_id=1605&page=809, accessed 21 April 2009.

37 United Nations Food and Agriculture Organization. "Gender and Food Security, Agriculture." Website: http://www.fao.org/gender/en/agri-e.htm, accessed 23 July 2009.

38 Scherr, S. J. and S. Sthapit. 2009. Capturing Carbon on the Land: Food, Land Use and Climate Change. Washington, D.C.: Worldwatch Institute.

39 Shandra, J. M., C. Shandra and B. London. 2008. "Women, Non-Governmental Organizations, and Deforestation: A Cross-National Study." *Population and Environment* 30: 48-72.

40 Ibid.

CHAPTER 3

1 Piguet, E. 2008. "Climate Change and Forced Migration," UNHCR Research Paper 153. Geneva.

2 Intergovernmental Panel on Climate Change. 1990. "Policy Maker Summary of Working Group II (Potential Impacts of Climate Change)," *First Assessment Report of the Intergovernmental Panel on Climate Change.* p. 103, para. 5.0.10.

3 Parry, M.L. and others. 2007. "Summary for Policymakers." *Climate Change 2007: Impacts, Adaptation and Vulnerability. Contribution of Working Group II to the Fourth Assessment Report of the Intergovernmental Panel on Climate Change.* Cambridge: Cambridge University Press.

4 Tacoli, C. 2009. "Crisis or Adaptation? Migration and Climate Change in a Context of High Mobility." *Environment and Urbanization* 21: 2.

5 Emergency Events Database (http://www.emdat.be) distinguishes between two categories of disasters: hydrometeorological disasters (avalanches/landslides, droughts/famines, extreme temperatures, floods, forest/scrub fires, windstorms and other disasters, such as insect infestations and wave surges) and geophysical disasters (earthquakes, tsunamis and volcanic eruptions). While there is no strict scientific definition of climatic disasters, the *World Disaster Report 2008* notes that climatic disasters are weather-related and include most of the hydrometeorological disasters, such as floods, cyclones, storms, extreme temperatures, drought, and wildfires, while avalanches, landslides and mudslides may be related to a mixture of climatic and geological factors. Geophysical disasters are generally not considered to be climate-related. Website: http://www.emdat.be, accessed 23 July 2009; International Federation of Red Cross and Red Crescent Societies. 2008. "World Disaster Report: Focus on HIV and AIDS," p.144. Website: http://www.preventionweb.net/files/2928_WDR2008full20reportLR.pdf, accessed 23 July 2009.

6 United Nations Office for the Coordination of Humanitarian Affairs. 2008. "Climate Change Risks Overwhelming Current Global Humanitarian Capacity," http://www.reliefweb.int/rw/rwb.nsf/db900sid/EDIS-7LYLUA?OpenDocument, accessed 23 July 2009.

7 Integrated Regional Information Networks. 2005. "Disaster Reduction and the Human Cost of Disaster," pp. 3 and 7. Website: http://www.irinnews.org/IndepthMain.aspx?IndepthId=14&ReportId=62446, accessed 23 July 2009.

8 Estimates based on Emergency Events Database figures given in Guha-Sapir, D., D. Hargitt and P. Hoyois. 2004. *Thirty Years of Natural Disasters 1974-2003: The Numbers.* Louvain: Presses Universitaires de Louvain. Website: http://www.emdat.be/Documents/Publications/publication_2004_emdat.pdf, accessed 23 July 2009.

9 http://ochaonline.un.org/News/InFocus/ClimateChange HumanitarianImpact/ClimateChangeIntroduction/VideoSlideshow/tabid/5100/language/en-US/Default.aspx, accessed 15 May 2009.

10 International Federation of Red Cross and Red Crescent Societies (2001). *World Disasters Report,* http://www.ifrc.org/publicat/wdr2001/, accessed 15 April, 2009; Conisbee, M. and Simms, A. (2003) *Environmental Refugees: The Case for Recognition.* London: New Economics Foundation.

11 Myers, N. 1993. "Environmental Refugees in a Globally Warmed World." BioScience, 43 (11): 757-761; Christian Aid. 2007. "Human Tide: The Real Migration Crisis."

12 Stern, N. 2006. "Part II: Impacts of Climate Change on Growth and Development." *The Economics of Climate Change: the Stern Review.* Cambridge: Cambridge University Press. Website: http://www.hm-treasury.gov.uk/d/Part_II_Introduction_group.pdf, accessed 27 July 2009.

13 Parry, M.L. and others. 2007. "Summary for Policymakers." *Climate Change 2007: Impacts, Adaptation and Vulnerability. Contribution of Working Group II to the Fourth Assessment Report of the Intergovernmental Panel on Climate Change.* Cambridge: Cambridge University Press.

14 International Organization for Migration. 2007. "Migration and the Environment." Discussion note MC/INF/288. Website: http://www.iom.int/jahia/webdav/site/myjahiasite/shared/shared/mainsite/microsites/IDM/workshops/evolving_global_economy_2728112007/MC_INF_288_EN.pdf, accessed 27 July 2009.

15 Kniveton, D. and others. 2008. *Climate Change and Migration: Improving Methodologies to Estimate Flows.* Migration Research Series No. 33. Geneva: International Organization for Migration.

16 Nicholls, R.J. and others. 2007. "Coastal Systems and Low-lying Areas—Climate Change 2007: Impacts, Adaptation and Vulnerability." Contribution of Working Group II to the *Fourth Assessment Report of the Intergovernmental Panel on Climate Change.* Cambridge: Cambridge University Press.

17 Cecilia Tacoli. 2009. "Crisis or Adaptation? Migration and Climate Change in a Context of High Mobility." *Environment and Urbanization* 21 (2): October.

18 Parry, M.L. and others. 2007. "Summary for Policymakers." *Climate Change 2007: Impacts, Adaptation and Vulnerability.* Contribution of Working Group II to the Fourth Assessment Report of the Intergovernmental Panel on Climate Change. Cambridge: Cambridge University Press.

19 de Kalbermatten, Grégoire G. 2008. "Desertification, Land Degradation and Drought as Push Factors of Forced Migrations", address to the United Nations Convention to Combat Desertification. http://www.iom.int/jahia/webdav/shared/mainsite/events/docs/hsn/hsn_address_kalbermatten.pdf, accessed 27 July 2009.

20 International Organization for Migration. 2008. "Expert Seminar: Migration and the Environment." *International Dialogue on Migration No. 10.* Geneva: International Organization for Migration.

21 Ibid.

22 Permanent Mission of Greece to the United Nations Office in Geneva and the International Organization for Migration, 2007. "Climate Change, Environmental Degradation and Migration: Addressing Vulnerabilities and Harnessing Opportunities." Background Paper. Website: http://www.iom.int/jahia/webdav/shared/shared/mainsite/events/docs/hsn_background_paper.pdf, accessed 27 July 2009.

23 Seck, E. 1996. "Désertification: effets, lutte et convention." Dossier documentaire. Dakar: ENDA-Tiers Monde.

24 Ibid. p.7.

25 Brody, A., J. Demetriades, and E. Esplen, 2008. "Gender and Climate Change: Mapping the Linkages." *A Scoping Study on Knowledge and Gaps,* Sussex: BRIDGE, Institute of Development Studies, University of Sussex.

26 Women's Commission for Refugee Women and Children. 2006. "Minimum Initial Service Package for Reproductive Health in Crisis Situations." Website: http://misp.rhrc.org, accessed 27 July 2009.

27 World Bank. 2007. "Dhaka: Improving Living Conditions for the Urban Poor." *Bangladesh Development Series.* Paper No. 17, Dhaka: World Bank

28 World Bank. 2009. "Urban Growth: A Challenge and an Opportunity." http://web.worldbank.org/WBSITE/EXTERNAL/COUNTRIES/SOUTHASIAEXT/0,,contentMDK:21393869-pagePK:146736-piPK:146830-theSitePK:223547,00.html#example, accessed 27 July 2009.

29 International Organization for Migration. 2008. "Expert Seminar: Migration and the Environment." *International Dialogue on Migration No. 10.* Geneva: International Organization for Migration.

30 International Organization for Migration. 2009. "Return of Skills." Website: http://www.iom.int/jahia/Jahia/about-migration/developing-migration-policy/migration-dvlpment/return-skills/cache/offonce%3Bjsessionid=EA68730B19165D5668FC9797E19FB275.worker02, accessed 27 July 2009; Development Research Centre on Migration, Globalisation and Poverty. 2005. "Report on the International Workshop on Sustainable Return of Professional and Skilled Migrants," 7-8 March.

31 Cecilia Tacoli. 2009. "Crisis or Adaptation? Migration and Climate Change in a Context of High Mobility." *Environment and Urbanization* 21 (2): October.

32 International Organization for Migration. 2007. "Migration, Development and Natural Disasters: Insights from the Indian Ocean Tsunami." *Migration Research Series:* 30; International Organization for Migration. 2008. "Migration and Climate Change." *Migration Research Series:* 31. Geneva.

CHAPTER 4

1 Women's Environment and Development Organization. 2008. "Final Report: Gender and Climate Change Workshop," 2-3 June. Website: http://www.wedo.org/wp-content/uploads/finalreport-dakar-workshop-2008.pdf, accessed 27 July 2009.

2 Rowling, M. 2008. "Women Farmers Toil to Expand Africa's Food Supply." Reuters. 26 December. Website: http://in.reuters.com/article/worldNews/idINIndia-37187320081226, accessed 27 July 2009.

3 United Nations Department of Economic and Social Affairs, Population Division. 2009. *World Population Prospects: 2008 Revision.* New York: United Nations.

4 Schuemer-Cross, T. and B. H. Taylor. 2009. *The Right to Survive: The Humanitarian Challenge for the 21st Century.* Oxford: Oxfam.

5 Alley, R.B., et al. 2007. "Summary for Policymakers." Climate Change 2007: The Physical Science Basis. Contribution of Working Group I to the Fourth Assessment Report of the Intergovernmental Panel on Climate Change. Cambridge: Cambridge University Press. Website: http://www.ipcc.ch/pdf/assessment-report/ar4/wg1/ar4-wg1-spm.pdf, accessed 27 July 2009.

6 McGranahan, G. and others. 2007. "The Rising Tide: Assessing the Risks of Climate Change and Human Settlements in Low-Elevation Coastal Zones." *Environment and Urbanization,* 19 (1): April.

7 Gray, D. 2007. "Cities at Risk of Rising Sea Levels." Associated Press, 30 October.

8 United Nations. 2005. *Seminar on the Relevance of Population Aspects for the Achievement of the Millennium Development Goals.* New York: United Nations. p. XII-1.

9 Cometto, G. 2009. "A Global Fund for the Health MDGs?" *The Lancet* 373 (9674): 1500-1502.

10 Parry, M.L. and others. 2007. "Summary for Policymakers." Climate Change 2007: *Impacts, Adaptation and Vulnerability.* Contribution of Working Group II to the Fourth Assessment Report of the *Intergovernmental Panel on Climate Change.* Cambridge: Cambridge University Press.

11 Le Blank, D. and R. Perez. 2008. "The Relationship Between Rainfall and Human Density and Its Implications for Future Water Stress in Sub-Saharan Africa." *Ecological Economics* 66: 319-336.

12 Paolisso, M. and S. Gammage. 1996. *Population, Poverty, and Women's Responses to Environmental Degradation: Case Studies from Latin America.* Washington, D.C.: International Center for Research on Women.

13 Women's Environment and Development Organization. 2008. "Final Report: Gender and Climate Change Workshop," 2-3 June. Website: http://www.wedo.org/wp-content/uploads/finalreport-dakar-workshop-2008.pdf, accessed 27 July 2009.

14 Asian Development Bank. 2001. "Country Briefing Paper: Women in Bangladesh." Manila: Asian Development Bank. Cited in Cannon, T. "Gender and Climate Hazards in Bangladesh." In Masika, R. (ed.). 2002. *Gender, Development, and Climate Change.* Oxford: Oxfam.

15 Neumayer, E., and T. Plümper. 2007. "The Gendered Nature of Natural Disasters: The Impact of Catastrophic Events on the Gender Gap in Life Expectancy, 1981–2002." *Annals of the Association of American Geographers* 97(3): 551–566.

16 Haider, R., A. A. Rahman and S. Huq. 1993. *Cyclone '91: An Environmental and Perceptional Study.* Dhaka: Bangladesh Centre for Advanced Studies.

17 Fothergill, A. "The Neglect of Gender in Disaster Work: An Overview of the Literature." In Enarson, E. and B. Hearn Morrow. 1998. *The Gendered Terrain of Disaster: Through Woman's Eyes.* Westport: Praeger.

18 Confalonieri, U. and B. Menne. 2007. "Human Health." In Parry, M.L. and others. 2007. "Summary for Policymakers— Climate Change 2007: Impacts, Adaptation and Vulnerability." Contribution of Working Group II to the *Fourth Assessment Report of the Intergovernmental Panel on Climate Change,* Cambridge: Cambridge University Press.

19 Pincha, C. Undated. *Understanding Gender Differential Impacts of Tsunami & Gender Mainstreaming Strategies in Tsunami Response in Tamilnadu, India.* Oxfam. Website: http://www.gdnonline.org/resources/Gender_mainstreaming_Pincha_etal.pdf, accessed 2 May 2009.

20 United Nations Population Fund. 2005. "Reproductive Health Care Being Restored in Tsunami-Hit Areas." Press release. 22 December; Caribbean Red Cross Societies. 2008. "Jamaica Red Cross, UNFPA Address Hygiene Needs After Gustav." Press release. Website: http://www.reliefweb.int/rw/rwb.nsf/db900sid/EDIS-7JRLDG?OpenDocument, accessed 27 July 2009. Regional Office of the Western Pacific. Undated. "Reproductive Health Kit for Emergency Situations." World Health Organization. Website: http://www.wpro.who.int/NR/rdonlyres/C90B674C-DD8E-4DAD-8248-E255D309C864/0/RHkit.pdf, accessed 2 May 2009.

21 Hynes, M. and others. 2002. "Reproductive Health Indicators and Outcomes Among Refugees and Internally Displaced Persons in Postemergency Phase Camps." *Journal of the American Medical Association* 288(5): 595-603.

22 World Bank. 2007. *Global Monitoring Report 2007: Confronting the Challenges of Gender Equality and Fragile States.* Washington, D.C.: The World Bank.

23 Ban, K. 2007. "A Climate Culprit in Darfur." *The Washington Post.* 16 June, p. A15. Website: http://www.washingtonpost.com/wp-dyn/content/article/2007/06/15/AR2007061501857.html, accessed 27 July 2009.

24 Dabelko, G. D. 2008. "Environmental Security Heats Up." *ECSP Report* 13:viii-x.

25 UN Habitat. 2009. "Cities and Climate Change Initiative." PowerPoint presentation, Bonn climate change conference, April 2009; Center for International Earth Sciences Information Network, Columbia University, and the Institute for Environment and Development. 2007. In Roy, S. 2007. "Climate Change: Coastal Mega-Cities in for a Bumpy Ride." 28 March. Inter Press News Service.

26 Epstein, P. R., and E. Mills (eds). 2005 (2nd printing 2006). *Climate Change Futures: Health, Ecological and Economic Dimensions.* Cambridge: Center for Health and the Global Environment, Harvard Medical School. p. 6.

27 Demick, B. 2009. "China Blames Pollution for Surge of Birth Defects." *Los Angeles Times.* 2 February; BBC. 2009. "China Birth Defects 'Up Sharply'."1 February.

28 Confaloniere, U. and Menne, B. 2007. "Impacts, Adaptation and Vulnerability." Contribution of Working Group II to the *Fourth Assessment Report of the Intergovernmental Panel on Climate Change.* Cambridge: Cambridge University Press.

29 Parry, M.L. and others. 2007. "Summary for Policymakers." *Climate Change 2007: Impacts, Adaptation and Vulnerability. Contribution of Working Group II to the Fourth Assessment Report of the Intergovernmental Panel on Climate Change.* Cambridge: Cambridge University Press.

30 Molden, D. and others. "Trends in Water and Agricultural Development." In International Water Management Institute. 2007. *Water for Food, Water for Life.* London: Earthscan and Colombo: International Water Management Institute.

31 World Bank. 2007. *Global Monitoring Report 2007: Confronting the Challenges of Gender Equality and Fragile States.* Washington, D.C.: The World Bank.

CHAPTER 5

1   Sen, A. 1993. "Capability and Oldrup, H. and M. H. Breengaard. 2009. "Gender and Climate Changes Report." Nordic Summit Declaration, Abstract—Desk Study on Gender Equality, and Climate Changes. Nordic Council of Ministers.

2   Raworth, K. 2008. "Coping With Climate Change: What Works for Women?" Factsheet. Oxfam GB. June. Website: http://www.oxfam.org.uk/resources/policy/climate_change/climate_change_women.html, accessed 5 May 2009; Awuor, C. B. 2009. "Impacts of and Adaptation to Climate Change." Presentation at congressional briefing "Disaster and Displacement: The Human Face of Climate Change." CARE

and Population Resource Center. 11 February. Washington, D.C.

3   Nyoni, S. 1993. *Women and Energy: Lessons from the Zimbabwe Experience.* Working Paper 22. Harare: Zimbabwe Environment Research Organization. Cited in Clancy J., M. Skutch and S. Batchelor. 2003. *The Gender-Energy-Poverty Nexus.* London: United Kingdom: Department for International Development. Cited in Brody, A., J. Demetriades and E. Esplen. 2008. *Gender and Climate Change: Mapping the Linkages, a Scoping Study on Knowledge and Gaps.* London: United Kingdom: Department for International Development.

4   Sengupta, S. 2009. "An Empire for Poor Working Women, Guided by a Gandhian Approach." *The New York Times.* 7 March. p. A6.

5   Wamukonya, N. and M. Skutsch. 2001. "Is There a Gender Angle to the Climate Change Negotiations?" Paper prepared for ENERGIA for the Commission on Sustainable Development, Session 9. New York, 16-27 April. Cited in Dankelman, I. 2002. "Climate Change: Learning from Gender Analysis and Women's Experiences of Organising for Sustainable Development." In Masika, R. (ed.). 2002. *Gender, Development, and Climate Change.* Oxford: Oxfam.

6   Engelman, R. 2008. *More: Population, Nature, and What Women Want.* Washington, D.C.: Island Press.

7   Byravan, S. 2008. *Gender and Innovation in South Asia.* International Development Research Centre. Website: http://www.idrc.ca/uploads/user-S/12215918981Byravan.pdf , accessed 5 May 2009.

8   Danish Agency for Science, Technology and Innovation. 2007. *Innovation og mangfoldighed – Ny viden og erfaringer med medar-bejderdreven innovation.* Cited in Oldrup, H. and M. H. Breengaard. 2009. "Gender and Climate Changes Report." Nordic Summit Declaration, Abstract—Desk Study on Gender Equality, and Climate Changes. Nordic Council of Ministers.

9   Terry, G. 2009. "No Climate Justice Without Gender Justice: An Overview of the Issues." Gender & Development 17(1): 5-18; Rosenwald, M.S. 2008. "Why He Jumps In and She Tests

the Water." *The Washington Post.* 17 August. p. F1.

10 Sullivan, K., and M. Jordan. 2009. "In Banking Crisis, Guys Get the Blame." *The Washington Post.* 11 February. p. A10.

11 ActionAid. 2008. "Women in Malawi Adapt to Climate Change." Website: http://us.oneworld.net/article/357923-women%E2%80%99s-network-malawi-adapts-climate-change, accessed 23 July 2009.

12 International Strategy for Disaster Reduction. 2008. *Gender Perspectives: Integrating Disaster Risk Reduction into Climate Change Adaptation, Good Practices and Lessons Learned.* Geneva: United Nations International Strategy for Disaster Reduction.

13 Anam, T. 2008. "Losing the Ground Beneath Their Feet." *The Guardian.* 4 September,p. 6; Dankelman, I. 2002. "Climate Change: Learning from Gender Analysis and Women's Experiences of Organizing for Sustainable Development." Gender and Development 10(2) July,

14 International Strategy for Disaster Reduction. 2008. *Gender Perspectives: Integrating Disaster Risk Reduction into Climate Change Adaptation, Good Practices and Lessons Learned.* Geneva: United Nations International Strategy for Disaster Reduction.

15 United Nations. 2008. *The Millennium Development Goals Report 2008.* New York: United Nations Department of Economic and Social Affairs, p. 19.

16 Goetz, A. M. and others. *Progress of the World's Women 2008/2009: Who Answers to Women? Gender and Accountability.* New York: United Nations Development Fund for Women (UNIFEM), p. 17.

17 Brody, A., Demetriades, J. and Esplen E. 2008. "Gender and Climate Change: Mapping the Linkages." *A Scoping Study on Knowledge and Gaps,* Sussex: BRIDGE, Institute of Development Studies, University of Sussex, p. 17.

18 Commission on Sustainable Development NGO Women's Caucus. Undated. Website : http://www.earthsummit2002.org/wcaucus/delegations.html, accessed 7 May 2009.

19   Dankelman, I. 2002. "Climate Change: Learning from Gender Analysis and Women's Experiences of Organizing for Sustainable Development." *Gender and Development* 10(2) July.

20   United Nations. 1992. *Agenda 21*. Website: http://www.un.org/esa/sustdev/documents/agenda21/english/agenda21toc.htm, accessed 7 May 2009.

21   World Women's Congress for a Healthy Planet. 1991. "Women's Action Agenda 21." Website: http://www.iisd.org/women/action21.htm, accessed 27 July 2009.

22   United Nations. 1994. "Report of the International Conference on Population and Development." Document A/CONF.171/13. Website: http://www.un.org/popin/icpd/conference/offeng/poa.html, accessed 27 July 2009.

23   United Nations Population Fund. 2004. *Investing in People: National Progress in Implementing the ICPD Programme of Action 1994-2004*. New York: UNFPA.

24   Guttmacher Institute. 2003. *Adding It Up: The Benefits of Investing in Sexual and Reproductive Health Care*. New York: Guttmacher Institute. Website: http://www.unfpa.org/upload/lib_pub_file/240_filename_addingitup.pdf, accessed 29 July 2009.

25   Obaid, T.A. 2009. "ICPD at 15: Putting People First. Statement to the United Nations Commission on Population and Development, New York, March 30.

26   Lutz, W. 2008. "It's Human Capital, Stupid!" *Popnet* 40: 1.

27   Engelman, R. 2009. "Population & Sustainability." *Scientific American Earth 3.0* (Summer) 19(2): 22-29.

28   Cohen, J. E. 2008. "Make Secondary Education Universal." *Nature* 456(4): 572-573.

29   United Nations Population Fund. 2005. *State of World Population 2005: The Promise of Equality*. New York: United Nations Population Fund.

CHAPTER 6

1   Beller, K. and H. Chase. 2008. *Great Peacemakers: True Stories from Around the World*. Sedona, Ariz.: LTS Press. p. 169.

2   Chakravartya, S. and others. 2009. "Sharing Global CO$_2$ Emission Reductions Among One Billion High Emitters." *Proceedings of the National Academy of Sciences* (PNAS Early Edition): Website: http://www.pnas.org_cgi_doi_10.1073_pnas.0905232106, accessed July 9, 2009; Baer, P. and others. 2008. *The Greenhouse Development Rights Framework: The Right to Development in a Climate Constrained World* (Second Edition). Berlin: Heinrich BÐll Stiftung.

3   Rogner, H-H. and others. 2007. *Climate Change 2007: Mitigation. Contribution of Working Group III to the Fourth Assessment Report of the Intergovernmental Panel on Climate Change*. (Metz, B. and others, eds.) Cambridge: Cambridge University Press. p. 109.

4   Speidel, J.J. and others. 2009. *Making the Case for U.S. International Family Planning Assistance*. Baltimore: Gates Institute, Johns Hopkins School of Public Health.

5   United Nations Department of Economic and Social Affairs, Population Division. 2009. *World Population Prospects: the 2008 Revision*. New York: United Nations.

6   Asian Forum of Parliamentarians for Population and Development. 2008. "Hanoi Statement of Commitment." Arising from the 9th AFPPD General Assembly on Addressing Climate Change and Food Security: Linking Population as a Factor, 13-14 December 2008.

7   Sinding, S.W., J.A. Ross and A. Rosenfield. 1994. "Seeking Common Ground: Unmet Need and Demographic Goals." *International Family Planning Perspectives* 20: 23-27, 32.

8   Potts, M. 1997. "Sex and the Birth Rate: Human Biology, Demographic Change, and Access to Fertility-Regulation Methods." *Population and Development Review* 23(1): 1-39.

9   UNAIDS. 2008. *Report on the Global HIV/AIDS Pandemic 2008* (Chapter 7, figure 7.1). Geneva: UNAIDS.

10   United Nations Department of Economic and Social Affairs, Population Division. 2009. *World Population Prospects: the 2008 Revision*. New York: United Nations.

11   Speidel, J.J. and others. 2009. *Making the Case for U.S. International Family Planning Assistance*. Baltimore: Gates Institute, Johns Hopkins School of Public Health.

12   Population Council. 1997. "South African Apartheid Spurred Women to Adopt Contraception." Press release. December. New York: The Population Council.

13   Sen, A. 1994. "Indian State Cuts Population without Coercion." Letter to *The New York Times*. 4 January.

14   United Nations Population Fund. 2009. "Flow of Financial Resources for Assisting in the Implementation of the Programme of Action of the International Conference on Population and Development." Report to the Commission on Population and Development, Forty-second Session, 30 March-3 April. E/CN.9/2009/5. New York: United Nations.

15   Guttmacher Institute. 2003. *Adding It Up: The Benefits of Investing in Sexual and Reproductive Health Care*. New York: Guttmacher Institute. Website: http://www.unfpa.org/upload/lib_pub_file/240_filename_addingitup.pdf, accessed 3 April 2009.

16   Lakshminarayanan, R. and others. 2007. *Population Issues in the 21st Century: The Role of the World Bank*. Washington, D.C.: World Bank.

17   Sadik, N. 2009. Address at United Nations Foundation, 23 April, Washington, D.C.

18   Deen, T. 2009. "Population: Global Financial Crisis Threatens Family Planning." 1 April. Inter Press News Service.

19   Women's Environment and Development Organization. 2008. "Final Report: Gender and Climate Change Workshop," 2-3 June. Website: http://www.wedo.org/wp-content/uploads/finalreport-dakar-workshop-2008.pdf, accessed 27 July 2009.

20   This section draws significantly from recommendations of the Women's Environment and Development Organization, GenderCC and the Global Gender and Climate Change Alliance, a consortium of WEDO, the International Union for the Conservation of Nature, the United Nations Environment Programme and the United Nations Development Programme.

21   Office of the United Nations High Commissioner for Human Rights. 2009. *Report of the Office of the United Nations High Commissioner for Human Rights on the Relationship Between Climate Change and Human Rights* (advance unedited version). New York: United Nations. A/HRC/10/61. 15 January.

Monitoring ICPD goals:
selected indicators

Country, territory or other area	Mortality			Education				Reproductive health			
	Infant mortality Total per 1,000 live births	Life expectancy M/F	Maternal mortality ratio	Primary enrolment (gross) M/F	Proportion reaching grade 5 M/F	Secondary enrolment (gross) M/F	% Illiterate (>15 years) M/F	Births per 1,000 women ages 15-19	Contraceptive Prevalence Any method	Modern methods	HIV prevalence rate (%) ages 15-49
Afghanistan	154	44.3 / 44.3	1,800	125 / 78		39 / 15		121	19	16	
Albania	15	73.7 / 80.0	92	106 / 105		78 / 75	.7 / 1.2	14	60	22	
Algeria	29	71.2 / 74.1	180	113 / 106	95 / 98	80 / 86	15.7 / 33.6	7	61	52	0.1
Angola	114	45.6 / 49.6	1,400	207 / 191				124	6	5	2.1
Argentina	13	71.8 / 79.4	77	115 / 113	95 / 97	79 / 89	2.4 / 2.3	57	65	64	0.5
Armenia	24	70.6 / 77.1	76	108 / 111		87 / 92	.3 / .7	36	53	19	0.1
Australia [1]	4	79.4 / 84.0	4	108 / 107		152 / 145		15	71	71	0.2
Austria	4	77.5 / 82.8	4	102 / 101		103 / 100		13	51	47	0.2
Azerbaijan	42	68.2 / 72.8	82	116 / 115		91 / 87	.2 / .8	34	51	13	0.2
Bahamas	9	71.2 / 76.7	16	103 / 103	96 / 100	92 / 96		53			
Bahrain	10	74.5 / 77.7	32	120 / 119	100 / 98	100 / 104	9.6 / 13.6	17	62	31	
Bangladesh	42	65.5 / 67.7	570	88 / 95	52 / 58	42 / 45	41.3 / 52	72	56	48	
Barbados	10	74.6 / 80.0	16	105 / 105	94 / 95	102 / 105		43			
Belarus	9	63.6 / 75.5	18	98 / 96		94 / 97	.2 / .3	21	73	56	0.2
Belgium	4	77.0 / 83.0	8	103 / 103	96 / 97	112 / 108		8	75	73	0.2
Belize	16	74.7 / 78.6	52	124 / 122	87 / 88	76 / 82		79	34	31	
Benin	82	60.7 / 63.0	840	105 / 87	72 / 71	41 / 23	46.9 / 72.1	112	17	6	1.2
Bhutan	42	64.7 / 68.4	440	103 / 101	91 / 95	51 / 46	35 / 61.3	38	31	31	
Bolivia (Plurinational State of)	43	63.9 / 68.2	290	108 / 108	83 / 83	83 / 81	4 / 14	78	61	34	0.2
Bosnia and Herzegovina	13	72.7 / 77.9	3	101 / 94		84 / 87		16	36	11	<0.1
Botswana	34	55.1 / 54.8	380	108 / 106	80 / 85	75 / 78	17.2 / 17.1	52	44	42	23.9
Brazil	22	69.1 / 76.4	110	134 / 125		95 / 105	10.2 / 9.8	76	77	70	0.6
Brunei Darussalam	5	75.2 / 80.0	13	106 / 105	99 / 100	96 / 99	3.5 / 6.9	25			
Bulgaria	11	70.1 / 77.1	11	102 / 100		108 / 103	1.4 / 2.1	42	63	40	
Burkina Faso	79	52.0 / 54.7	700	71 / 60	78 / 82	18 / 13	63.3 / 78.4	131	17	13	1.6
Burundi	96	49.4 / 52.4	1,100	119 / 110	65 / 68	18 / 13		19	20	9	2.0
Cambodia	59	59.7 / 63.4	540	124 / 115	61 / 64	44 / 32	14.2 / 32.3	39	40	27	0.8
Cameroon	85	50.8 / 51.9	1,000	118 / 101	64 / 64	28 / 22		128	29	12	5.1
Canada	5	78.6 / 83.1	7	99 / 99		103 / 100		13	74	74	0.4
Cape Verde	24	68.7 / 74.1	210	105 / 98	89 / 94	73 / 86	10.6 / 21.2	95	61		
Central African Republic	103	45.9 / 48.8	980	84 / 58	61 / 57			107	19	9	6.3
Chad	128	47.7 / 50.3	1,500	87 / 61	41 / 34	26 / 12	57 / 79.2	164	3	2	3.5
Chile	7	75.7 / 81.9	16	108 / 103	98 / 98	90 / 92	3.4 / 3.5	60	64		0.3
China	22	71.6 / 75.1	45	113 / 112		77 / 78	3.5 / 10	10	87	86	0.1
Colombia	18	69.6 / 77.0	130	117 / 116	85 / 92	81 / 90	7.6 / 7.2	74	78	68	0.6
Comoros	46	63.6 / 68.1	400	91 / 80	80 / 81	40 / 30	19.7 / 30.2	46	26	19	

Country, territory or other area	Mortality			Education				Reproductive health			
	Infant mortality Total per 1,000 live births	Life expectancy M/F	Maternal mortality ratio	Primary enrolment (gross) M/F	Proportion reaching grade 5 M/F	Secondary enrolment (gross) M/F	% Illiterate (>15 years) M/F	Births per 1,000 women ages 15-19	Contraceptive Prevalence Any method	Modern methods	HIV prevalence rate (%) ages 15-49
Congo, Democratic Republic of the [2]	115	46.2 / 49.4	1,100	94 / 76		44 / 23		201	21	6	
Congo, Republic of	79	52.8 / 54.7	740	110 / 102	65 / 67	46 / 39		113	44	13	3.5
Costa Rica	10	76.7 / 81.5	30	111 / 110	86 / 89	85 / 90	4.3 / 3.8	67	80	72	0.4
Côte d'Ivoire	85	56.7 / 59.3	810	81 / 64	83 / 73	32 / 18		130	13	8	3.9
Croatia	6	73.1 / 79.8	7	99 / 99		90 / 93	.5 / 2	14			<0.1
Cuba	5	76.9 / 81.0	45	103 / 100	97 / 97	93 / 93	.2 / .2	45	73	72	0.1
Cyprus	5	77.5 / 82.2	10	103 / 102	100 / 100	97 / 99	1 / 3.4	6			
Czech Republic	4	73.7 / 79.8	4	101 / 100	98 / 99	95 / 96		11	72	63	
Denmark	4	76.3 / 80.9	3	99 / 99	100 / 100	118 / 121		6			0.2
Djibouti	82	54.4 / 57.2	650	50 / 43	93 / 87	30 / 21		23	18	17	
Dominican Republic	28	70.0 / 75.6	150	110 / 103	66 / 71	72 / 87	11.2 / 10.5	109	73	70	1.1
Ecuador	20	72.4 / 78.3	210	119 / 118	80 / 83	69 / 70	12.7 / 18.3	83	73	58	0.3
Egypt	33	68.6 / 72.2	130	108 / 102	96 / 97	91 / 85	25.4 / 42.2	39	60	58	
El Salvador	20	66.8 / 76.3	170	118 / 118	72 / 76	63 / 66	15.1 / 20.3	83	73	66	0.8
Equatorial Guinea	97	49.5 / 51.8	680	128 / 121	34 / 31	41 / 23		123	10	6	
Eritrea	52	57.6 / 62.2	450	60 / 50	59 / 61	34 / 24	23.8 / 47	67	8	5	1.3
Estonia	7	68.0 / 78.7	25	100 / 98	97 / 97	99 / 101	.2 / .2	21	70	56	1.3
Ethiopia	77	54.3 / 57.1	720	97 / 85	64 / 65	37 / 24		104	15	14	2.1
Fiji	19	66.8 / 71.4	210	96 / 93	85 / 87	78 / 87		32			0.1
Finland	3	76.5 / 83.2	7	98 / 97	100 / 100	109 / 114		11			0.1
France	4	78.0 / 84.9	8	111 / 110	98 / 98	113 / 114		7	71		0.4
French Polynesia	8	72.3 / 77.2						52			
Gabon	49	59.7 / 62.2	520	153 / 152	68 / 71	53 / 46	9.8 / 17.8	90	33	12	5.9
Gambia	75	54.6 / 58.0	690	84 / 89	77 / 75	51 / 46		88	18	13	0.9
Georgia	33	68.3 / 75.2	66	100 / 98	86 / 90	90 / 90		45	47	27	0.1
Germany	4	77.4 / 82.6	4	104 / 104		101 / 99		8	70	66	0.1
Ghana	72	55.9 / 57.7	560	98 / 97	62 / 65	52 / 46	28.3 / 41.7	64	24	17	1.9
Greece	4	77.3 / 81.7	3	101 / 101	99 / 98	105 / 99	1.8 / 4	9	76	42	0.2
Guadeloupe	7	76.2 / 82.4					5 / 4.6	19			
Guam	9	73.5 / 78.2						52	67	58	
Guatemala	28	67.1 / 74.2	290	117 / 110	69 / 68	58 / 53	21 / 32	107	43	34	0.8
Guinea	95	56.4 / 60.4	910	98 / 84	87 / 79	48 / 27		152	9	4	1.6
Guinea-Bissau	111	46.7 / 49.8	1,100			23 / 13		129	10	6	1.8
Guyana	41	64.8 / 70.6	470	113 / 111	64 / 65	111 / 103		63	34	33	
Haiti	62	59.7 / 63.2	670				39.9 / 36	46	32	24	2.2
Honduras	27	70.1 / 74.9	280	120 / 119	81 / 87	57 / 71	16.3 / 16.5	93	65	56	0.7
Hong Kong SAR, China [3]	4	79.6 / 85.3		100 / 96	99 / 100	86 / 86		6	84	80	
Hungary	7	69.6 / 77.7	6	97 / 95		96 / 95	1 / 1.2	20	77	68	0.1
Iceland	3	80.4 / 83.5	4	97 / 98	98 / 100	108 / 114		15			
India	53	62.6 / 65.6	450	114 / 109	66 / 65	59 / 49	23.1 / 45.5	68	56	49	0.3

Country, territory or other area	Mortality — Infant mortality Total per 1,000 live births	Life expectancy M/F	Maternal mortality ratio	Education — Primary enrolment (gross) M/F	Proportion reaching grade 5 M/F	Secondary enrolment (gross) M/F	% Illiterate (>15 years) M/F	Reproductive health — Births per 1,000 women ages 15-19	Contraceptive Prevalence Any method	Modern methods	HIV prevalence rate (%) ages 15-49
Indonesia	25	69.2 / 73.2	420	120 / 115	92 / 94	73 / 74	4.8 / 11.2	40	61	57	0.2
Iran (Islamic Republic of)	28	70.3 / 73.1	140	106 / 137	88 / 88	83 / 78	12.7 / 22.8	18	73	59	0.2
Iraq	32	64.6 / 71.9	300	109 / 90	87 / 73	54 / 36		86	50	33	
Ireland	4	77.8 / 82.5	1	105 / 104	97 / 100	110 / 118		16	89	89	0.2
Israel	5	78.8 / 83.0	4	110 / 112	100 / 99	91 / 92		14			0.1
Italy	4	78.3 / 84.3	3	105 / 104	99 / 100	102 / 100	.9 / 1.4	5	60	39	0.4
Jamaica	23	68.8 / 75.5	170	91 / 92	88 / 93	87 / 92	19.5 / 8.9	77	69	66	1.6
Japan	3	79.4 / 86.5	6	100 / 100		101 / 101		5	54	44	
Jordan	18	71.1 / 74.9	62	95 / 97	97 / 96	88 / 91	4.8 / 13	25	57	41	
Kazakhstan	25	59.2 / 71.5	140	105 / 106		93 / 92	.2 / .5	31	51	49	0.1
Kenya	62	54.5 / 55.3	560	114 / 112	81 / 85	56 / 49		104	39	32	
Korea, Democratic People's Republic of	47	65.3 / 69.5	370					0	69	58	
Korea, Republic of	4	76.2 / 82.8	14	108 / 105	98 / 98	102 / 95		6	80		<0.1
Kuwait	9	76.2 / 80.1	4	100 / 97	100 / 99	90 / 92	4.8 / 6.9	13	52	39	
Kyrgyzstan	36	64.5 / 71.9	150	96 / 95		86 / 87	.5 / .9	32	48	46	0.1
Lao People's Democratic Republic	47	64.0 / 66.9	660	124 / 111	62 / 61	49 / 39	17.5 / 36.8	37	32	29	0.2
Latvia	9	67.8 / 77.5	10	96 / 93		98 / 99	.2 / .2	15	48	39	0.8
Lebanon	21	70.1 / 74.4	150	97 / 94	90 / 95	77 / 86	6.6 / 14	16	58	34	0.1
Lesotho	67	45.0 / 45.7	960	115 / 114	68 / 80	33 / 42		74	37	35	23.2
Liberia	93	57.3 / 60.1	1,200	96 / 87		37 / 27	39.8 / 49.1	142	11	10	1.7
Libyan Arab Jamahiriya	17	72.0 / 77.2	97	113 / 108		86 / 101	5.5 / 21.6	3	45	26	
Lithuania	9	66.1 / 77.9	11	96 / 95		98 / 98	.3 / .3	22	47	31	0.1
Luxembourg	4	77.1 / 82.3	12	102 / 103	98 / 100	96 / 99		12			
Madagascar	63	59.2 / 62.5	510	144 / 139	42 / 43	27 / 26		133	27	17	0.1
Malawi	80	52.9 / 54.7	1,100	114 / 119	44 / 43	31 / 26	20.8 / 35.4	135	41	38	11.9
Malaysia	9	72.3 / 77.0	62	98 / 98	92 / 92	66 / 72	5.8 / 10.4	13	55	30	0.5
Maldives	22	70.4 / 73.6	120	112 / 109	89 / 96	80 / 86	3 / 2.9	13	39	34	
Mali	104	48.1 / 49.2	970	92 / 74	83 / 80	39 / 25	65.1 / 81.8	163	8	6	1.5
Malta	6	78.0 / 81.6	8	101 / 99	99 / 100	99 / 100	8.8 / 6.5	12	86	46	
Martinique	7	76.8 / 82.5					3.1 / 4.7	30			
Mauritania	72	55.0 / 59.0	820	100 /106	63 / 65	27 / 24	36.7 / 51.7	90	9	8	0.8
Mauritius [4]	14	68.5 / 75.8	15	101 / 101	99 / 99	89 / 88	9.8 / 15.3	39	76	39	1.7
Melanesia [5]	45	61.0 / 65.4						51			
Mexico	16	74.1 / 79.0	60	116 / 112	94 / 96	88 / 90	5.6 / 8.6	65	71	67	0.3
Micronesia [6]	24	70.3 / 74.5						37			
Moldova, Republic of	18	64.9 / 72.5	22	95 / 94		87 / 90		34	68	43	0.4
Mongolia	41	63.8 / 70.2	46	99 / 101	86 / 83	87 / 97	3.2 / 2.3	17	66	61	0.1
Montenegro	8	72.0 / 76.7						15	39	17	
Morocco	29	69.4 / 73.9	240	113 / 101	85 / 83	60 / 51	31.3 / 56.8	19	63	52	0.1
Mozambique	86	47.4 / 48.8	520	119 / 103	68 / 60	21 / 16	42.8 / 67	149	17	12	12.5

Country, territory or other area	Mortality			Education				Reproductive health			
	Infant mortality Total per 1,000 live births	Life expectancy M/F	Maternal mortality ratio	Primary enrolment (gross) M/F	Proportion reaching grade 5 M/F	Secondary enrolment (gross) M/F	% Illiterate (>15 years) M/F	Births per 1,000 women ages 15-19	Contraceptive Prevalence Any method	Modern methods	HIV prevalence rate (%) ages 15-49
Myanmar	72	59.9 / 64.4	380		68 / 72			18	37	33	0.7
Namibia	32	60.8 / 62.4	210	110 / 109	97 / 99	54 / 64	11.4 / 12.6	74	55	54	15.3
Nepal	40	66.4 / 67.8	830	127 / 126	60 / 64	45 / 41	29.7 / 56.4	101	48	44	0.5
Netherlands	4	78.0 / 82.2	6	108 / 106	99 / 100	121 / 118		4	67	65	0.2
Netherlands Antilles	12	72.9 / 79.6		125 / 123	80 / 88	87 / 95	3.7 / 3.6	32			
New Caledonia	6	73.1 / 80.0					3.7 / 4.8	26			
New Zealand	4	78.5 / 82.4	9	101 / 102		119 / 123		23	74	71	0.1
Nicaragua	20	70.5 / 76.7	170	117 / 115	43 / 51	65 / 73	21.9 / 22.1	113	72	69	0.2
Niger	85	51.1 / 52.9	1,800	61 / 46	74 / 69	13 / 8	57.1 / 84.9	157	11	5	0.8
Nigeria	108	47.6 / 48.7	1,100	105 / 89	82 / 84	35 / 28	19.9 / 35.9	127	15	9	3.1
Norway	3	78.7 / 83.0	7	99 / 99	100 / 99	114 / 112		9	88	82	0.1
Occupied Palestinian Territory	17	72.1 / 75.3		80 / 80		90 / 95	2.8 / 9.7	79	50	39	
Oman	12	74.6 / 77.8	64	80 / 81	98 / 99	92 / 88	10.6 / 22.5	10	24	18	
Pakistan	62	66.5 / 67.2	320	101 / 83	68 / 72	37 / 28	32.3 / 60.4	46	30	22	0.1
Panama	17	73.3 / 78.5	130	114 / 111	90 / 91	68 / 73	6 / 7.2	83			1.0
Papua New Guinea	49	59.3 / 63.6	470	60 / 50			37.9 / 46.6	55	26	20	1.5
Paraguay	31	70.0 / 74.2	150	113 / 110	86 / 90	66 / 67	4.3 / 6.5	72	79	70	0.6
Peru	20	70.9 / 76.2	240	117 / 118	93 / 93	96 / 100	5.1 / 15.4	55	71	47	0.5
Philippines	22	69.9 / 74.4	230	110 / 109	73 / 81	79 / 87	6.9 / 6.3	45	51	36	
Poland	7	71.6 / 80.0	8	97 / 97		100 / 99	.4 / 1	14	49	19	0.1
Polynesia [7]	17	70.6 / 76.0						38			
Portugal	4	75.7 / 82.2	11	118 / 112		98 / 105	3.4 / 6.7	17	67	63	0.5
Puerto Rico	7	75.0 / 82.9	18					54	84	72	
Qatar	8	75.1 / 77.2	12	110 / 109	87 / 87	105 / 102	6.2 / 9.6	16	43	32	
Réunion	7	72.5 / 80.7					9.9 / 8.2	34	67	64	
Romania	14	69.5 / 76.5	24	105 / 104		88 / 87	1.7 / 3.1	31	70	38	0.1
Russian Federation	11	60.7 / 73.4	28	96 / 96		85 / 83	.3 / .6	25	73	53	1.1
Rwanda	97	48.8 / 52.5	1,300	146 / 149	43 / 49	19 / 17		37	36	26	2.8
Samoa	21	69.0 / 75.2		96 / 95	96 / 92	76 / 86	1.1 / 1.6	28	25	23	
Saudi Arabia	18	71.2 / 75.6	18	100 / 96		94 / 86	10.9 / 20.6	26	24		
Senegal	58	54.4 / 57.5	980	84 / 84	65 / 65	30 / 23	47.7 / 67	104	12	10	1.0
Serbia	11	71.9 / 76.6		97 / 97		87 / 89		22	41	19	0.1
Sierra Leone	102	46.7 / 49.2	2,100	155 / 139		38 / 26	50 / 73.2	126	8	6	1.7
Singapore	3	78.1 / 83.1	14				2.7 / 8.4	5	62	53	0.2
Slovakia	7	71.1 / 78.8	6	103 / 101		93 / 94		21	80	66	<0.1
Slovenia	4	74.9 / 82.2	6	104 / 103		94 / 94	.3 / .4	5	74	59	<0.1
Solomon Islands	42	65.7 / 68.0	220			33 / 27		42			
Somalia	107	48.7 / 51.5	1,400	16 / 9				70	15	1	0.5
South Africa	45	50.3 / 53.1	400	104 / 101	82 / 83	95 / 99	11.1 / 12.8	59	60	60	18.1
Spain	4	77.9 / 84.3	4	106 / 105	100 / 100	116 / 124	1.4 / 2.7	12	66	62	0.5

Country, territory or other area	Mortality			Education				Reproductive health			
	Infant mortality Total per 1,000 live births	Life expectancy M/F	Maternal mortality ratio	Primary enrolment (gross) M/F	Proportion reaching grade 5 M/F	Secondary enrolment (gross) M/F	% Illiterate (>15 years) M/F	Births per 1,000 women ages 15-19	Contraceptive Prevalence Any method	Modern methods	HIV prevalence rate (%) ages 15-49
Sri Lanka	15	70.6 / 78.1	58	108 / 108	93 / 94	86 / 88	7.3 / 10.9	30	68	53	
Sudan	67	57.0 / 60.1	450	71 / 61	72 / 69	35 / 32		57	8	6	1.4
Suriname	22	65.7 / 72.9	72	120 / 118	78 / 81	67 / 93	7.3 / 11.9	40	42	41	
Swaziland	62	47.1 / 45.5	390	118 / 109	76 / 88	58 / 51		84	51	47	26.1
Sweden	3	79.0 / 83.2	3	95 / 94	100 / 100	104 / 103		8	75	65	0.1
Switzerland	4	79.6 / 84.3	5	98 / 97		95 / 91		6	82	78	0.6
Syrian Arab Republic	15	72.5 / 76.4	130	129 / 123	93 / 92	73 / 71	10.3 / 23.5	61	58	43	
Tajikistan	59	64.5 / 69.7	170	102 / 98		91 / 76	.2 / .5	28	38	33	0.3
Tanzania, United Republic of	62	55.5 / 57.1	950	113 / 111	85 / 89		21 / 34.1	130	26	20	6.2
Thailand	7	66.1 / 72.2	110	106 / 106		79 / 88	4.1 / 7.4	37	81	80	1.4
The former Yugoslav Republic of Macedonia	14	72.0 / 76.8	10	95 / 95		85 / 83		22	14	10	<0.1
Timor-Leste, Democratic Republic of	63	60.7 / 62.5	380	94 / 88		53 / 54		54	10	7	
Togo	70	61.2 / 64.6	510	104 / 90	58 / 51	52 / 27		65	17	11	3.3
Trinidad and Tobago	25	66.1 / 73.2	45	101 / 99	90 / 92	83 / 89	.9 / 1.7	35	43	38	1.5
Tunisia	19	72.1 / 76.4	100	106 / 103	96 / 96	81 / 89	13.6 / 31	7	60	52	0.1
Turkey	26	69.7 / 74.6	44	99 / 93	100 / 94	88 / 72	3.8 / 18.7	39	71	43	
Turkmenistan	49	61.1 / 69.2	130				.3 / .7	20	62	45	<0.1
Uganda	72	52.8 / 54.1	550	116 / 117	49 / 49	25 / 20	18.2 / 34.5	150	24	18	5.4
Ukraine	12	63.0 / 73.9	18	100 / 100		94 / 94	.2 / .4	28	67	48	1.6
United Arab Emirates	9	76.9 / 79.0	37	107 / 106	100 / 100	91 / 94	10.5 / 8.5	16	28	24	
United Kingdom	5	77.4 / 81.8	8	104 / 104		96 / 99		24	82	82	0.2
United States of America	6	77.1 / 81.6	11	99 / 99	96 / 98	94 / 95		36	73	68	0.6
Uruguay	13	73.1 / 80.1	20	116 / 113	93 / 96	93 / 92	2.6 / 1.8	61	77	75	0.6
Uzbekistan	47	64.9 / 71.2	24	97 / 94		103 / 102		13	65	59	0.1
Vanuatu	27	68.7 / 72.6		110 / 106	72 / 72		20 / 23.9	47	39	32	
Venezuela (Bolivarian Republic of)	17	71.1 / 77.1	57	107 / 105	96 / 100	75 / 84	4.6 / 5.1	90	70	62	
Viet Nam	19	72.7 / 76.6	150		87 / 87	69 / 64		17	79	68	0.5
Yemen	56	61.8 / 65.1	430	100 / 74	67 / 65	61 / 30	23 / 59.5	68	28	19	
Zambia	90	45.8 / 46.9	830	121 / 117	94 / 84	46 / 41	19.2 / 39.3	142	41	27	15.2
Zimbabwe	54	45.3 / 45.6	880	102 / 101	68 / 71	42 / 39	5.9 / 11.7	65	60	58	15.3

World and regional data	Mortality			Education				Reproductive health			
	Infant mortality Total per 1,000 live births	Life expectancy M/F	Maternal mortality ratio	Primary enrolment (gross) M/F	Proportion reaching grade 5 M/F	Secondary enrolment (gross) M/F	% Illiterate (>15 years) M/F	Births per 1,000 women ages 15-19	Contraceptive Prevalence — Any method	Modern methods	HIV prevalence rate (%) ages 15-49
World Total	46	65.8 / 70.2	400	109 / 104		68 / 65	11.6 / 20.6	52	62	55	0.8
More developed regions *	6	73.9 / 80.8	9	101 / 101		98 / 98	0.5 / 0.8	21	69	58	0.5
Less developed regions +	51	64.3 / 67.8		110 / 104		63 / 60	14.4 / 26.2	57	61	55	1
Least developed countries ‡	80	55.3 / 57.8						103	27	21	3
Africa 8	80	53.5 / 55.8	820	104 / 94		43 / 36	27.6 / 45.3	103	28	22	4
Eastern Africa	74	53.0 / 55.0		108 / 103		33 / 27	31.1 / 48.9	111	26	20	5.8
Middle Africa 9	110	47.2 / 50.1		110 / 92		35 / 22	23 / 47.4	167	19	7	2.5
Northern Africa 10	40	66.6 / 70.2	160	101 / 93		65 / 63	23.8 / 42.9	32	50	44	0.3
Southern Africa	46	50.5 / 53.0	900	105 / 102		89 / 93	11.9 / 12.9	61	58	58	18.5
Western Africa 11	96	50.7 / 52.3		97 / 84		36 / 27	32.4 / 50.2	123	13	8	2.5
Arab States 12	39	67.1 / 70.8	240	99.8 / 90.2		71.6 / 65.2	18.9 / 37.4	42	46	40	0.5
Asia	40	67.5 / 71.2	330	110 / 106		67 / 62	12.2 / 23.7	40	67	61	0.2
Eastern Asia 13	21	72.4 / 76.6	50	111 / 111		79 / 80	3.2 / 8.7	9	86	85	0.1
South Central Asia	55	63.1 / 66.0		110 / 105		60 / 49	24.7 / 45	63	54	46	0.3
South-Eastern Asia	27	68.3 / 72.8	300	111 / 109		71 / 73	5.8 / 11.3	33	60	54	0.5
Western Asia	29	69.2 / 74.0	160	104 / 94		78 / 66	8.2 / 22	48			
Europe	7	71.5 / 79.4		103 / 102		98 / 98	0.6 / 1	17	69	56	0.5
Eastern Europe	11	64.2 / 75.0		98 / 98		90 / 89	0.4 / 0.8	24	64	44	0.9
Northern Europe 14	5	76.7 / 81.7		102 / 102		100 / 102	0.2 / 0.3	19	81	75	0.2
Southern Europe 15	5	76.9 / 82.9		106 / 104		102 / 103	1.3 / 2.6	11	63	46	0.4
Western Europe 16	4	77.7 / 83.4		107 / 106		107 / 105	0.4 / 0.4	7	77	74	0.2
Latin America & Caribbean	21	70.6 / 77.0	130	119 / 115		85 / 92	8.3 / 9.7	72	71	64	0.5
Caribbean 17	34	69.4 / 74.5		107 / 104		68 / 73	13.3 / 11.8	65	62	55	1.1
Central America	18	72.9 / 78.2		116 / 113		81 / 84	8.2 / 11.6	74	68	63	0.4
South America 18	20	69.9 / 76.9		122 / 117		89 / 97	7.8 / 8.7	73	73	66	0.6
Northern America 19	6	77.3 / 81.7		99 / 99		95 / 95	0.2 / 0.2	34	73	69	0.6
Oceania	22	74.4 / 79.1	430	93 / 90		145 / 141	6.4 / 7.6	28		59	0.4
Australia-New Zealand	4	79.3 / 83.7		107 / 106		145 / 141	0 / 0	16			

Demographic, social and economic indicators

Country, territory or other area	Total population (millions) (2009)	Projected population (millions) (2050)	Ave. pop. growth rate (%) (2005-2010)	% urban (2009)	Urban growth rate (2005-2010)	Population/ ha arable &-perm. crop land	Total fertility rate (2009)	% births with skilled attendants	GNI per capita PPP$ (2007)	Expenditures/ primary student (% of GDP per capita)	Health expenditures, public (% of GDP)	External population assistance (US$,000)	Under-5 mortality M/F estimates (2005-2010)	Per capita energy consumption	Access to improved drinking water sources
Afghanistan	28.2	73.9	3.4	24	5.2	2.0	6.51	14				48,360	233 / 238		22
Albania	3.2	3.3	0.4	47	1.8	2.0	1.85	100	7,240		2.4	4,062	18 / 17	715	97
Algeria	34.9	49.6	1.5	66	2.5	0.9	2.34	95	7,640		3.4	1,811	35 / 31	1,100	85
Angola	18.5	42.3	2.7	58	4.4	3.2	5.64	47	4,270	3.7	2.3	25,739	220 / 189	620	51
Argentina	40.3	50.9	1.0	92	1.2	0.1	2.22	99	12,970	12.0	4.6	7,176	17 / 14	1,766	96
Armenia	3.1	3.0	0.2	64	0.1	0.7	1.75	98	5,870		1.9	5,344	29 / 25	859	98
Australia [1]	21.3	28.7	1.1	89	1.3	0.0	1.84	99	33,400	17.3	5.9	(99,319)	6 / 5	5,917	100
Austria	8.4	8.5	0.4	67	0.7	0.2	1.39	100	36,750	23.5	7.7	(7,996)	6 / 5	4,132	100
Azerbaijan	8.8	10.6	1.1	52	1.4	1.0	2.15	89	6,570		1.1	4,090	54 / 52	1,659	78
Bahamas	0.3	0.5	1.2	84	1.5	0.8	2.00	99			3.6	0	14 / 12		97
Bahrain	0.8	1.3	2.1	89	2.1	1.0	2.23	99			2.5	0	13 / 13	11,874	
Bangladesh	162.2	222.5	1.4	28	3.3	9.2	2.29	18	1,330		1.0	79,053	58 / 56	161	80
Barbados	0.3	0.2	0.3	40	1.5	0.6	1.54	100			4.2	362	12 / 10		100
Belarus	9.6	7.3	-0.5	74	0.1	0.2	1.28	100	10,750	14.4	4.8	3,898	14 / 9	2,939	100
Belgium	10.6	11.5	0.5	97	0.6	0.2	1.78	99	35,320	20.2	7.2	(55,963)	6 / 5	5,782	
Belize	0.3	0.5	2.1	52	3.1	0.8	2.84	96	6,080		2.6	527	23 / 19		91
Benin	8.9	22.0	3.2	42	4.2	1.4	5.38	78	1,310	13.4	2.4	13,329	123 / 118	321	65
Bhutan	0.7	1.0	1.7	36	5.3	2.8	2.56	51	4,980		2.5	2,530	69 / 59		81
Bolivia (Plurinational State of)	9.9	14.9	1.8	66	2.5	0.7	3.37	66	4,150		4.0	15,447	65 / 56	625	86
Bosnia and Herzegovina	3.8	3.0	-0.1	48	1.1	0.1	1.21	100	8,020		5.2	4,946	17 / 12	1,427	99
Botswana	2.0	2.8	1.5	60	2.8	2.6	2.82	94	12,880	16.1	5.4	45,435	60 / 47	1,054	96
Brazil	193.7	218.5	1.0	86	1.5	0.4	1.83	97	9,270	15.4	3.6	7,718	33 / 25	1,184	91
Brunei Darussalam	0.4	0.7	1.9	75	2.5	0.3	2.05	100	50,200		1.5		7 / 6	7,346	
Bulgaria	7.5	5.4	-0.6	71	-0.2	0.1	1.44	99	11,100	24.5	4.1	3,355	17 / 13	2,688	99
Burkina Faso	15.8	40.8	3.4	20	5.7	2.2	5.84	54	1,120	36.0	3.6	34,995	160 / 154		72
Burundi	8.3	14.8	2.9	11	5.9	5.5	4.45	34	330	19.9	0.7	10,494	177 / 155		71
Cambodia	14.8	23.8	1.6	22	4.6	2.4	2.86	44	1,720		1.5	54,407	92 / 85	351	65
Cameroon	19.5	36.7	2.3	58	3.8	1.2	4.54	63	2,120	7.6	1.0	35,825	151 / 136	390	70
Canada	33.6	44.4	1.0	81	1.1	0.0	1.58	100	35,500		7.0	(231,143)	6 / 6	8,262	100
Cape Verde	0.5	0.7	1.4	60	2.7	1.9	2.66	78	2,940		3.8	953	38 / 23		80
Central African Republic	4.4	7.6	1.9	39	2.4	1.4	4.70	54	710	7.5	1.5	1,133	196 / 163		66
Chad	11.2	27.8	2.8	27	4.7	1.3	6.08	14	1,280	7.1	2.6	3,935	220 / 201		48
Chile	17.0	20.7	1.0	89	1.3	1.3	1.93	100	12,300	11.1	2.8	5,218	10 / 8	1,812	95
China	1,345.8	1,417.0	0.6	44	2.8	5.6	1.77	98	5,420		1.9	78,604	25 / 35	1,433	88
Colombia	45.7	62.9	1.5	75	1.9	2.4	2.40	96	8,260	15.6	6.2	3,773	30 / 22	695	93
Comoros	0.7	1.2	2.3	28	2.5	4.3	3.89	62	1,150		1.8	25,172	71 / 54		85

Country, territory or other area	Total population (millions) (2009)	Projected population (millions) (2050)	Ave. pop. growth rate (%) (2005-2010)	% urban (2009)	Urban growth rate (2005-2010)	Population/ha arable &-perm. crop land	Total fertility rate (2009)	% births with skilled attendants	GNI per capita PPP$ (2007)	Expenditures/primary student (% of GDP per capita)	Health expenditures, public (% of GDP)	External population assistance (US$,000)	Under-5 mortality M/F estimates (2005-2010)	Per capita energy consumption	Access to improved drinking water sources
Congo, Democratic Republic of the [2]	66.0	147.5	2.8	35	4.7	4.8	5.91	74	290		1.3	47,699	209 / 187	289	46
Congo, Republic of	3.7	6.9	1.9	62	2.6	2.4	4.27	86	2,750	3.0	1.5	3,648	135 / 122	327	71
Costa Rica	4.6	6.4	1.4	64	2.3	1.6	1.94	94	10,510		5.3	1,456	13 / 10	1,040	98
Côte d'Ivoire	21.1	43.4	2.3	50	3.7	1.2	4.51	57	1,620		0.9	45,687	129 / 117	385	81
Croatia	4.4	3.8	-0.2	58	0.3	0.3	1.44	100	15,540		7.1	237	8 / 7	2,017	99
Cuba	11.2	9.7	0.0	76	0.1	0.4	1.51	100		51.1	7.1	12,059	9 / 6	944	91
Cyprus	0.9	1.2	1.0	70	1.3	0.4	1.52	100	24,040		2.8	0	7 / 6	3,094	100
Czech Republic	10.4	10.3	0.4	74	0.4	0.2	1.45	100	22,690	12.6	6.1	75	5 / 4	4,485	100
Denmark	5.5	5.6	0.2	87	0.6	0.1	1.85		36,800	25.1	9.3	(138,992)	6 / 6	3,850	100
Djibouti	0.9	1.5	1.8	88	2.3	479.2	3.79	93	2,260		5.0	4,607	134 / 116		92
Dominican Republic	10.1	13.4	1.4	70	2.5	1.0	2.61	98	6,350	10.3	2.1	16,224	37 / 29	816	95
Ecuador	13.6	18.0	1.1	66	2.1	1.3	2.51	99	7,110		2.3	11,694	29 / 22	851	95
Egypt	83.0	129.5	1.8	43	1.9	6.8	2.82	79	5,370		2.6	48,792	42 / 39	843	98
El Salvador	6.2	7.9	0.4	61	1.0	2.2	2.30	84	5,640	9.0	4.1	6,814	29 / 23	697	84
Equatorial Guinea	0.7	1.4	2.6	40	3.0	1.5	5.28	63	21,220		1.7	1,157	177 / 160		43
Eritrea	5.1	10.8	3.1	21	5.4	5.5	4.53	28	620	9.6	1.7	10,061	78 / 71	150	60
Estonia	1.3	1.2	-0.1	70	-0.1	0.2	1.69	100	18,830	19.4	3.8	2,836	11 / 8	3,638	100
Ethiopia	82.8	173.8	2.6	17	4.5	4.5	5.21	6	780	12.5	2.3	334,223	138 / 124	289	42
Fiji	0.8	0.9	0.6	53	1.6	1.2	2.69	99	4,240		2.6	719	25 / 24		47
Finland	5.3	5.4	0.4	64	0.9	0.1	1.84	100	34,760	18.0	6.2	(38,829)	5 / 4	7,108	100
France	62.3	67.7	0.5	78	0.8	0.1	1.88	99	33,850	17.4	8.8	(307,194)	5 / 4	4,444	100
French Polynesia	0.3	0.4	1.3	52	1.3	3.1	2.18	100				0	10 / 10		
Gabon	1.5	2.5	1.8	86	2.4	0.8	3.24	86	13,410		3.3	3,069	85 / 75	1,391	87
Gambia	1.7	3.8	2.7	57	4.4	3.6	4.97	57	1,140		2.8	3,404	123 / 109		86
Georgia	4.3	3.3	-1.1	53	-1.0	1.3	1.58	98	4,760		1.8	10,716	39 / 33	754	99
Germany	82.2	70.5	-0.1	74	0.1	0.1	1.32	100	34,740	16.3	8.2	(193,151)	5 / 5	4,231	100
Ghana	23.8	45.2	2.1	51	3.7	1.9	4.22	50	1,320	18.4	1.7	70,247	119 / 115	413	80
Greece	11.2	10.9	0.2	61	0.6	0.3	1.39		27,830	14.1	5.9	(12,188)	5 / 4	2,792	100
Guadeloupe	0.5	0.5	0.5	98	0.5	0.4	2.10	99					10 / 8		
Guam	0.2	0.2	1.3	93	1.3	3.8	2.49	87					11 / 10		
Guatemala	14.0	27.5	2.5	49	3.5	2.5	4.02	41	4,520	10.5	1.7	18,159	45 / 34	628	96
Guinea	10.1	24.0	2.3	35	3.7	2.7	5.33	38	1,120		0.8	5,846	157 / 138		70
Guinea-Bissau	1.6	3.6	2.2	30	2.5	2.4	5.66	39	470		1.5	2,516	207 / 186		57
Guyana	0.8	0.6	-0.1	28	0.1	0.3	2.30	83	2,580		5.1	19,462	66 / 47		93
Haiti	10.0	15.5	1.6	48	4.7	4.6	3.42	26	1,050		5.7	116,948	90 / 80	272	58
Honduras	7.5	12.4	2.0	48	3.0	1.4	3.19	67	3,610		3.1	19,061	44 / 35	621	84
Hong Kong SAR, China [3]	7.0	8.6	0.5	100	0.5		1.01	100	43,940	12.5			5 / 4	2,653	
Hungary	10.0	8.9	-0.2	68	0.4	0.2	1.37	100	17,470	25.7	5.9	0	9 / 8	2,740	100
Iceland	0.3	0.4	2.1	92	2.2	3.0	2.09		34,070		7.5		4 / 4	14,237	100
India	1,198.0	1,613.8	1.4	30	2.4	3.5	2.68	47	2,740	8.9	0.9	139,007	77 / 86	510	89

Demographic, social and economic indicators

Country, territory or other area	Total population (millions) (2009)	Projected population (millions) (2050)	Ave. pop. growth rate (%) (2005-2010)	% urban (2009)	Urban growth rate (2005-2010)	Population/ ha arable &-perm. crop land	Total fertility rate (2009)	% births with skilled attendants	GNI per capita PPP$ (2007)	Expenditures/ primary student (% of GDP per capita)	Health expenditures, public (% of GDP)	External population assistance (US$,000)	Under-5 mortality M/F estimates (2005-2010)	Per capita energy consumption	Access to improved drinking water sources
Indonesia	230.0	288.1	1.2	53	3.4	2.5	2.13	73	3,570		1.3	43,821	37 / 27	803	80
Iran (Islamic Republic of)	74.2	97.0	1.2	69	2.0	0.9	1.78	97	10,840	15.4	3.4	2,325	33 / 35	2,438	94
Iraq	30.7	64.0	2.2	66	2.0	0.4	3.96	89			2.7	44,197	43 / 38		77
Ireland	4.5	6.3	1.8	62	2.3	0.3	1.95	100	37,700	14.7	5.9	(121,018)	6 / 6	3,628	
Israel	7.2	10.6	1.7	92	1.7	0.4	2.75		26,310	20.7	4.5	78	6 / 5	3,017	100
Italy	59.9	57.1	0.5	68	0.7	0.2	1.39	99	30,190	23.1	6.9	(38,317)	5 / 4	3,125	
Jamaica	2.7	2.7	0.5	54	0.9	1.8	2.36	97	5,300	14.6	2.5	7,021	28 / 28	1,724	93
Japan	127.2	101.7	-0.1	67	0.2	0.7	1.26	100	34,750	22.2	6.6	(313,695)	5 / 4	4,129	100
Jordan	6.3	10.2	3.0	79	3.1	2.0	3.02	99	5,150	15.4	4.2	4,361	24 / 19	1,294	98
Kazakhstan	15.6	17.8	0.7	58	1.2	0.1	2.29	100	9,600		2.3	4,232	34 / 26	4,012	96
Kenya	39.8	85.4	2.6	22	4.1	4.6	4.86	42	1,550	22.4	2.2	239,215	112 / 95	491	57
Korea, Democratic People's Republic of	23.9	24.6	0.4	63	1.0	2.1	1.85	97			3.0	330	63 / 63	913	100
Korea, Republic of	48.3	44.1	0.4	82	0.7	1.6	1.22	100	24,840	18.8	3.6	0	6 / 6	4,483	92
Kuwait	3.0	5.2	2.4	98	2.5	1.6	2.15	100		9.2	1.7	0	11 / 9	9,729	
Kyrgyzstan	5.5	6.9	1.2	36	1.7	0.9	2.52	98	1,980		2.8	8,466	49 / 42	542	89
Lao People's Democratic Republic	6.3	10.7	1.8	32	5.8	3.5	3.42	20	2,080	9.1	0.7	7,364	68 / 61		60
Latvia	2.2	1.9	-0.5	68	-0.4	0.2	1.43	100	15,790		3.9	7	12 / 10	2,017	99
Lebanon	4.2	5.0	0.8	87	1.0	0.4	1.84	98	10,040	8.3	3.9	4,179	31 / 21	1,173	100
Lesotho	2.1	2.5	0.9	26	3.8	2.5	3.26	55	1,940	25.0	4.0	20,814	112 / 96		78
Liberia	4.0	8.8	4.1	61	5.4	3.8	5.01	46	280	6.0	1.2	10,544	144 / 136		64
Libyan Arab Jamahiriya	6.4	9.8	2.0	78	2.3	0.1	2.64	100	14,710		1.6	1,539	20 / 19	2,943	71
Lithuania	3.3	2.6	-1.0	67	-0.8	0.2	1.37	100	16,830	15.9	4.3	0	14 / 9	2,517	
Luxembourg	0.5	0.7	1.2	82	1.0	0.1	1.67	100			6.6	(28,896)	6 / 6	9,972	100
Madagascar	19.6	42.7	2.7	30	3.9	3.9	4.62	51	930	9.5	2.0	14,475	105 / 95		47
Malawi	15.3	36.6	2.8	19	5.6	3.2	5.46	54	760		8.9	119,991	125 / 117		76
Malaysia	27.5	39.7	1.7	71	3.1	0.5	2.51	100	13,230		1.9	98	12 / 10	2,617	99
Maldives	0.3	0.5	1.4	39	5.1	5.4	2.00	84	4,910		6.5	1,454	31 / 26		83
Mali	13.0	28.3	2.4	33	4.3	1.3	5.41	49	1,040	21.3	2.9	39,870	193 / 188		60
Malta	0.4	0.4	0.4	95	0.6	0.5	1.25	100	22,460		6.5		7 / 7	2,153	100
Martinique	0.4	0.4	0.4	98	0.4	0.7	1.89	100					8 / 8		
Mauritania	3.3	6.1	2.4	41	3.0	3.2	4.39	61	2,000	9.6	1.5	4,621	128 / 112		60
Mauritius [4]	1.3	1.4	0.7	43	0.8	1.2	1.79	99	11,410	10.3	2.0	1,197	20 / 15		100
Melanesia [5]	8.6	15.6	2.2	19	2.4		3.80	46					64 / 62		
Mexico	109.6	129.0	1.0	78	1.4	0.8	2.16	94	13,910	15.1	2.9	7,654	22 / 18	1,702	95
Micronesia [6]	0.6	0.8	1.3	68	1.6		2.47	87					33 / 26		
Moldova, Republic of	3.6	2.7	-1.0	41	-1.6	0.3	1.50	100	2,800	33.6	4.4	6,781	26 / 21	884	90
Mongolia	2.7	3.4	1.2	57	1.4	0.6	1.99	99	3,170	14.9	4.2	4,822	49 / 40	1,080	72
Montenegro	0.6	0.6	0.0	60	-0.5	0.5	1.64	99	11,780		6.0	2,163	11 / 9		98
Morocco	32.0	42.6	1.2	56	1.9	1.1	2.33	63	4,050	14.6	1.4	17,323	43 / 29	458	83
Mozambique	22.9	44.1	2.3	38	4.6	3.2	4.97	48	730	15.1	3.5	199,056	162 / 144	420	42

Country, territory or other area	Total population (millions) (2009)	Projected population (millions) (2050)	Ave. pop. growth rate (%) (2005-2010)	% urban (2009)	Urban growth rate (2005-2010)	Population/ha arable &perm. crop land	Total fertility rate (2009)	% births with skilled attendants	GNI per capita PPP$ (2007)	Expenditures/primary student (% of GDP per capita)	Health expenditures, public (% of GDP)	External population assistance (US$,000)	Under-5 mortality M/F estimates (2005-2010)	Per capita energy consumption	Access to improved drinking water sources
Myanmar	50.0	63.4	0.9	33	2.9	2.9	2.28	57			0.3	8,085	120 / 102	295	80
Namibia	2.2	3.6	1.9	37	3.6	1.1	3.29	81	5,100	21.4	3.8	85,019	58 / 45	721	93
Nepal	29.3	49.0	1.8	18	4.9	9.0	2.82	19	1,060	15.3	1.6	24,483	52 / 55	340	89
Netherlands	16.6	17.4	0.4	82	1.1	0.4	1.75	100	39,470	17.7	7.5	(552,546)	6 / 5	4,901	100
Netherlands Antilles	0.2	0.2	1.5	93	1.8	0.1	1.96					0	16 / 12	9,161	
New Caledonia	0.3	0.4	1.5	65	2.1	6.5	2.06	92					9 / 8		
New Zealand	4.3	5.3	0.9	87	1.1	0.3	2.03	94	25,380	17.8	7.2	(13,848)	6 / 5	4,192	97
Nicaragua	5.7	8.1	1.3	57	1.8	0.4	2.68	74	2,510	9.8	4.6	36,732	29 / 22	624	79
Niger	15.3	58.2	3.9	17	4.4	0.7	7.07	18	630	28.7	3.2	18,167	171 / 173		42
Nigeria	154.7	289.1	2.3	49	3.9	1.0	5.17	35	1,760		1.1	236,978	190 / 184	726	47
Norway	4.8	5.9	0.9	78	1.0	0.2	1.89		53,650	18.9	7.3	(264,920)	5 / 4	5,598	100
Occupied Palestinian Territory	4.3	10.3	3.2	72	3.4	1.7	4.92	97				11,237	23 / 18		
Oman	2.8	4.9	2.1	72	2.2	8.3	2.98	98		15.1	1.9	30	14 / 13	6,057	82
Pakistan	180.8	335.2	2.2	37	3.4	3.5	3.87	39	2,540		0.3	75,584	85 / 94	499	90
Panama	3.5	5.1	1.6	74	2.8	0.9	2.52	91	10,610	12.4	5.0	341	27 / 20	845	92
Papua New Guinea	6.7	12.9	2.4	13	2.3	5.4	4.01	39	1,870		2.6	42,741	70 / 68		40
Paraguay	6.3	9.9	1.8	61	2.8	0.5	2.98	77	4,520		2.9	5,340	44 / 32	660	77
Peru	29.2	39.8	1.2	72	1.3	1.7	2.53	73	7,200	7.0	2.6	24,499	38 / 27	491	84
Philippines	92.0	146.2	1.8	66	3.0	3.1	3.03	60	3,710	8.6	1.3	43,396	32 / 21	498	93
Poland	38.1	32.0	-0.1	61	-0.2	0.5	1.27	100	15,500	23.7	4.3	10	9 / 7	2,562	
Polynesia [7]	0.7	0.8	0.8	43	1.4		2.93	100					22 / 19		
Portugal	10.7	10.0	0.3	60	1.4	0.7	1.38	100	21,790	23.2	7.2	(5,778)	6 / 5	2,402	99
Puerto Rico	4.0	4.1	0.4	99	0.7	0.8	1.83	100				8	9 / 8		
Qatar	1.4	2.3	10.7	96	11.3	0.3	2.36	100			3.4	0	10 / 10	22,057	100
Réunion	0.8	1.1	1.3	94	1.7	0.5	2.41						10 / 8		
Romania	21.3	17.3	-0.4	54	-0.1	0.2	1.33	99	12,350	10.7	3.5	6,101	20 / 15	1,860	88
Russian Federation	140.9	116.1	-0.4	73	-0.4	0.1	1.39	100	14,330		3.3	49,460	18 / 14	4,745	97
Rwanda	10.0	22.1	2.7	19	4.2	4.9	5.33	52	860	10.2	4.6	105,790	167 / 143		65
Samoa	0.2	0.2	-0.0	23	0.9	0.7	3.85	100	4,350		4.2	334	28 / 25		88
Saudi Arabia	25.7	43.7	2.1	82	2.4	0.4	3.04	96	22,950	18.5	2.5	386	26 / 17	6,170	89
Senegal	12.5	26.1	2.6	43	3.3	2.9	4.89	52	1,650	17.9	3.3	23,125	125 / 114	250	77
Serbia	9.9	9.2	0.0	52	0.4	0.4	1.61	99	9,830		5.7	2,163	15 / 13	2,303	99
Sierra Leone	5.7	12.4	2.7	38	3.6	3.5	5.17	42	660		1.5	8,591	160 / 136		53
Singapore	4.7	5.2	2.5	100	2.5	5.0	1.26	100	47,950	9.3	1.1	0	4 / 4	6,968	
Slovakia	5.4	4.9	0.1	57	0.3	0.3	1.30	100	19,220	14.8	5.0	0	9 / 8	3,465	100
Slovenia	2.0	2.0	0.2	48	-0.4	0.1	1.39	100	26,230	25.1	6.1	40	5 / 4	3,618	
Solomon Islands	0.5	1.0	2.5	18	4.3	4.6	3.78	43	1,710		4.7	1,923	56 / 57		70
Somalia	9.1	23.5	2.3	37	3.6	5.0	6.35	33			0.0	8,747	186 / 174		29
South Africa	50.1	56.8	1.0	61	1.8	0.4	2.51	91	9,450	15.6	3.0	284,019	79 / 64	2,739	93
Spain	44.9	51.3	1.0	77	1.2	0.1	1.47		30,750	19.1	6.0	(139,496)	5 / 5	3,277	100

Country, territory or other area	Total population (millions) (2009)	Projected population (millions) (2050)	Ave. pop. growth rate (%) (2005-2010)	% urban (2009)	Urban growth rate (2005-2010)	Population/ ha arable &-perm. crop land	Total fertility rate (2009)	% births with skilled atten- dants	GNI per capita PPP$ (2007)	Expen- ditures/ primary student (% of GDP per capita)	Health expendi- tures, public (% of GDP)	External population assistance (US$,000)	Under-5 mortality M/F estimates (2005-2010)	Per capita energy consump- tion	Access to improved drinking water sources
Sri Lanka	20.2	21.7	0.9	15	0.9	4.4	2.31	99	4,200		2.0	2,354	21 / 18	472	82
Sudan	42.3	75.9	2.2	44	4.4	1.1	4.06	49	1,880		1.4	22,058	117 / 104	470	70
Suriname	0.5	0.6	1.0	75	1.4	1.3	2.37	90	7,640		2.6	4,725	35 / 26		92
Swaziland	1.2	1.7	1.3	25	2.5	1.8	3.45	74	4,890	15.4	4.1	20,019	111 / 92		60
Sweden	9.2	10.6	0.5	85	0.6	0.1	1.87		37,490	25.7	7.5	(366,182)	4 / 4	5,650	100
Switzerland	7.6	8.5	0.4	74	0.5	1.0	1.46	100	44,410	24.5	6.4	(36,974)	6 / 5	3,770	100
Syrian Arab Republic	21.9	36.9	3.3	55	4.0	0.9	3.17	93	4,430	20.3	1.9	2,257	21 / 16	975	89
Tajikistan	7.0	11.1	1.6	27	1.7	2.3	3.35	83	1,710	9.4	1.1	8,704	83 / 74	548	67
Tanzania, United Republic of	43.7	109.5	2.9	26	4.7	2.8	5.52	46	1,200		3.7	223,909	112 / 100	527	55
Thailand	67.8	73.4	0.7	34	1.7	1.5	1.82	97	7,880		2.3	45,477	13 / 8	1,630	98
The former Yugoslav Republic of Macedonia	2.0	1.9	0.1	67	0.8	0.4	1.44	98	9,050		5.6	2,535	17 / 16	1,355	100
Timor-Leste, Democratic Republic of	1.1	3.2	3.3	28	5.0	3.8	6.38	19	3,090	27.6	15.2	3,611	92 / 91		62
Togo	6.6	13.2	2.5	43	4.2	1.4	4.17	62	770	9.8	1.3	12,703	105 / 91	375	59
Trinidad and Tobago	1.3	1.3	0.4	14	3.0	2.1	1.65	98	22,420		2.5	1,253	37 / 28	10,768	94
Tunisia	10.3	12.7	1.0	67	1.6	0.5	1.84	90	7,140	20.9	2.3	7,030	24 / 21	863	94
Turkey	74.8	97.4	1.2	69	2.0	0.8	2.10	83	12,810		3.5	29,925	36 / 27	1,288	97
Turkmenistan	5.1	6.8	1.3	49	2.3	0.8	2.43	100			2.5	156	72 / 56	3,524	
Uganda	32.7	91.3	3.3	13	4.5	3.0	6.25	42	1,040		1.8	251,540	129 / 116		64
Ukraine	45.7	35.0	-0.7	68	-0.6	0.2	1.36	99	6,810	15.8	3.8	39,200	18 / 13	2,937	97
United Arab Emirates	4.6	8.3	2.8	78	2.9	0.5	1.90	100		4.4	1.8	0	10 / 12	11,036	100
United Kingdom	61.6	72.4	0.5	90	0.6	0.2	1.85	99		18.9	7.2	(1,137,342)	6 / 6	3,814	100
United States of America	314.7	403.9	1.0	82	1.3	0.0	2.08	99	45,840	22.2	7.0	(3,065,842)	7 / 8	7,768	99
Uruguay	3.4	3.6	0.3	92	0.4	0.3	2.09	99	11,020	8.8	3.6	437	18 / 15	962	100
Uzbekistan	27.5	36.4	1.1	37	1.2	1.4	2.25	100	2,430		2.4	8,646	63 / 53	1,829	88
Vanuatu	0.2	0.5	2.5	25	4.4	0.7	3.88	93	3,410		2.7	698	39 / 29		59
Venezuela (Bolivarian Republic of)	28.6	42.0	1.7	94	2.1	0.6	2.50	95	12,290	9.1	2.4	677	24 / 19	2,302	89
Viet Nam	88.1	111.7	1.1	28	2.9	5.9	2.03	88	2,530		2.1	60,877	27 / 20	621	92
Yemen	23.6	53.7	2.9	31	4.9	5.9	5.10	36	2,200		2.1	27,065	84 / 73	326	66
Zambia	12.9	29.0	2.4	36	2.9	0.9	5.74	47	1,190	2.3	3.8	166,147	169 / 152	625	58
Zimbabwe	12.5	22.2	0.3	38	1.6	2.3	3.36	69			4.5	75,608	100 / 88	724	81

Demographic, social and economic indicators

World and regional data	Total population (millions) (2009)	Projected population (millions) (2050)	Ave. pop. growth rate (%) (2005-2010)	% urban (2009)	Urban growth rate (2005-2010)	Population/ha arable &-perm. crop land	Total fertility rate (2009)	% births with skilled attendants	GNI per capita PPP$ (2007)	Expenditures/primary student (% of GDP per capita)	Health expenditures, public (% of GDP)	External population assistance (US$,000)	Under-5 mortality M/F estimates (2005-2010)	Per capita energy consumption	Access to improved drinking water sources
World Total	**6,829.4**	**9,150.0**	**1.2**	**50**	**2.0**		**2.54**	**66**	**9,947**			**8,766,710**	**71 / 71**	**1,820**	
More developed regions [*]	**1,233.3**	**1,275.2**	**0.3**	**75**	**0.6**		**1.64**	**99**					**8 / 7**		
Less developed regions [+]	**5,596.1**	**7,875.0**	**1.4**	**45**	**2.6**		**2.70**	**62**					**78 / 78**		
Least developed countries [‡]	**835.5**	**1,672.4**	**2.3**	**29**	**4.1**		**4.29**	**38**	**1,171**				**138 / 126**	**309**	
Africa [8]	**1,009.9**	**1,998.5**	**2.3**	**40**	**3.4**		**4.52**	**49**				**3,179,335**	**142 / 130**		
Eastern Africa	318.8	711.4	2.6	23	4.1		5.17	35				1,790,256	131 / 117		
Middle Africa [9]	125.7	273.0	2.6	42	4.2		5.53	63				122,771	200 / 178		
Northern Africa [10]	209.4	321.1	1.7	52	2.5		2.84	73				98,552	60 / 52		
Southern Africa	57.5	67.4	1.0	58	1.9		2.59	89				455,307	80 / 65		
Western Africa [11]	298.6	625.6	2.5	44	3.9		5.14	42				531,575	169 / 162		
Arab States [12]	**352.2**	**598.2**	**2.1**	**56**	**2.5**		**3.30**	**73**				**235,412**	**57.8 / 50.7**		
Asia	**4,121.1**	**5,231.5**	**1.1**	**42**	**2.5**		**2.32**	**65**				**971,340**	**56 / 61**		
Eastern Asia [13]	1,555.4	1,600.0	0.6	48	2.3		1.73	98				83,756	24 / 33		
South Central Asia	1,754.6	2,493.7	1.5	32	2.5		2.74	45				405,355	78 / 85		
South-Eastern Asia	582.7	766.0	1.2	47	3.1		2.28	73				267,137	41 / 32		
Western Asia	228.4	371.8	1.9	66	2.4		2.89	81				143,866	40 / 33		
Europe	**732.2**	**691.1**	**0.1**	**72**	**0.3**		**1.51**	**99**					**10 / 8**		
Eastern Europe	292.5	240.0	-0.4	68	-0.3		1.37	99				108,880	16 / 12		
Northern Europe [14]	98.4	112.5	0.5	84	0.6		1.83	99					6 / 6		
Southern Europe [15]	153.1	153.7	0.5	67	0.9		1.46	99				19,019	7 / 6		
Western Europe [16]	188.2	184.9	0.2	77	0.5		1.59	100					5 / 5		
Latin America & Caribbean	**582.4**	**729.2**	**1.1**	**79**	**1.6**		**2.21**	**90**				**394,650**	**31 / 24**		
Caribbean [17]	42.0	49.5	0.8	66	1.6		2.35	73				154,273	48 / 41		
Central America	151.3	196.8	1.2	71	1.6		2.39	83				90,745	27 / 21		
South America [18]	389.1	482.9	1.1	83	1.6		2.12	94				106,168	31 / 24		
Northern America [19]	**348.4**	**448.5**	**1.0**	**82**	**1.3**		**2.03**	**99**					**7 / 7**		
Oceania	**35.4**	**51.3**	**1.3**	**71**	**1.4**		**2.43**	**77**				**50,249**	**31 / 30**		
Australia-New Zealand	25.6	34.1	1.0	89	1.2		1.87	98					6 / 5		

Notes for indicators

* More-developed regions comprise North America, Japan, Europe and Australia-New Zealand.

\+ Less-developed regions comprise all regions of Africa, Latin America and Caribbean, Asia (excluding Japan), and Melanesia, Micronesia and Polynesia.

‡ Least-developed countries according to standard United Nations designation.

1 Including Christmas Island, Cocos (Keeling) Islands and Norfolk Island.

2 Formerly Zaire.

3 On 1 July 1997, Hong Kong became a Special Administrative Region (SAR) of China.

4 Including Agalesa, Rodrigues and St. Brandon.

5 Including New Caledonia and Vanuatu.

6 Comprising Federated States of Micronesia, Guam, Kiribati, Marshall Islands, Nauru, Northern Mariana Islands, and Pacific Islands (Palau).

7 Comprising American Samoa, Cook Islands, Johnston Island, Pitcairn, Samoa, Tokelau, Tonga, Midway Islands, Tuvalu, and Wallis and Futuna Islands.

8 Including British Indian Ocean Territory and Seychelles.

9 Including Sao Tome and Principe.

10 Including Western Sahara.

11 Including St. Helena, Ascension and Tristan da Cunha.

12 Comprising Algeria, Bahrain, Comoros, Djibouti, Egypt, Iraq, Jordan, Kuwait, Lebanon, Libyan Arab Jamahiriya, Mauritania, Morocco, Occupied Palestinian Territory, Oman, Qatar, Saudi Arabia, Somalia, Sudan, Syria, Tunisia, United Arab Emirates and Yemen. Regional aggregation for demographic indicators provided by the UN Population Division. Aggregations for other indicators are weighted averages based on countries with available data.

13 Including Macau.

14 Including Channel Islands, Faeroe Islands and Isle of Man.

15 Including Andorra, Gibraltar, Holy See and San Marino.

16 Including Leichtenstein and Monaco.

17 Including Anguilla, Antigua and Barbuda, Aruba, British Virgin Islands, Cayman Islands, Dominica, Grenada, Montserrat, Netherlands Antilles, Saint Kitts and Nevis, Saint Lucia, Saint Vincent and the Grenadines, Turks and Caicos Islands, and United States Virgin Islands.

18 Including Falkland Islands (Malvinas) and French Guiana.

19 Including Bermuda, Greenland, and St. Pierre and Miquelon.

Technical notes

The statistical tables in *The State of World Population* give special attention to indicators that can help track progress in meeting the quantitative and qualitative goals of the International Conference on Population and Development (ICPD) and the Millennium Development Goals (MDGs) in the areas of mortality reduction, access to education, access to reproductive health services including family planning, and HIV and AIDS prevalence among young people. The sources for the indicators and their rationale for selection follow, by category.

Monitoring ICPD goals

Indicators of mortality

Infant mortality, male and female life expectancy at birth. Source: United Nations, Department of Economic and Social Affairs, Population Division (United Nations Population Division). These indicators are measures of mortality levels, respectively, in the first year of life (which is most sensitive to development levels) per 1,000 live births and over the entire lifespan. Data estimates are for 2009.

Maternal mortality ratio. Source: World Health Organization (WHO), UNICEF, UNFPA and World Bank. 2007. *Maternal Mortality in 2005: Estimates Developed by WHO, UNICEF, UNFPA and The World Bank.* Geneva: WHO. This indicator presents the estimated number of deaths to women per 100,000 live births which result from conditions related to pregnancy, delivery, the postpartum period, and related complications. Estimates between 100-999 are rounded to the nearest 10; and above 1,000 to the nearest 100. Several of the estimates differ from official government figures. The estimates are based on reported figures wherever possible, using approaches that improve the comparability of information from different sources. See the source for details on the origin of particular national estimates. Estimates and methodologies are reviewed regularly by WHO, UNICEF, UNFPA, academic institutions and other agencies and are revised where necessary, as part of the ongoing process of improving maternal mortality data. Because of changes in methods, prior estimates for 1995 and 2000 may not be strictly comparable with these estimates. Maternal mortality estimates reported here are based on the global database on maternal mortality, which is updated every 5 years. The last update for 2005, reported here, was published in 2007.

Indicators of education

Male and female gross primary enrolment ratios, male and female gross secondary enrolment ratios. Source: UNESCO Institute for Statistics, April 2009. Population data are based on: United Nations Population Division. 2009. *World Population Prospects: The 2008 Revision.* New York: United Nations. Gross enrolment ratios indicate the number of students enrolled in a level in the education system per 100 individuals in the appropriate age group. They do not correct for individuals who are older than the level-appropriate age due to late starts, interrupted schooling or grade repetition. Data are for the most recent year estimates available for the 1999-2007 period.

Male and female adult illiteracy. Source: See gross enrolment ratios above for source; data adjusted to illiteracy from literacy. Illiteracy definitions are subject to variation in different countries; three widely accepted definitions are in use. Insofar as possible, data refer to the proportion who cannot, with understanding, both read and write a short simple statement on everyday life. Adult illiteracy (rates for persons above 15 years of age) reflects both recent levels of educational enrolment and past educational attainment. The above education indicators have been updated using estimates from: United Nations Population Division. 2009. *World Population Prospects: The 2008 Revision.* New York: United Nations. Data are for the most recent year estimates available for the 1995-2007 period.

Proportion reaching grade 5 of primary education. Source: See gross enrolment ratios above for source. Data are most recent within the school years 1999-2007.

Indicators of reproductive health

Births per 1,000 women aged 15-19. Source: United Nations Population Division. This is an indicator of the burden of fertility on young women. Since it is an annual level summed over all women in the age cohort, it does not reflect fully the level of fertility for women during their youth. Since it indicates the annual average number of births per woman per year, one could multiply it by five to approximate the number of births to 1,000 young women during their late teen years. The measure does not indicate the full dimensions of teen pregnancy as only live births are included in the numerator. Stillbirths and spontaneous or induced abortions are not reflected. Estimates are for the 2005-2010 period.

Contraceptive prevalence. Source: United Nations Population Division. *World Contraceptive Use 2009.* These data are derived from sample survey reports and estimate the pro-

portion of married women (including women in consensual unions) currently using, respectively, any method or modern methods of contraception. Modern or clinic and supply methods include male and female sterilization, IUD, the pill, injectables, hormonal implants, condoms and female barrier methods. These numbers are roughly but not completely comparable across countries due to variation in the timing of the surveys and in the details of the questions. All country and regional data refer to women ages 15-49. The most recent survey data available are cited, ranging from 1986-2008. Indicators in World and Regional Listing section provided by Population Reference Bureau 2008 World Population Data Sheet.

HIV prevalence rate, ages 15-49. Source: The World Bank. *World Development Indicators 2009.* These data derive from surveillance system reports and model estimates. Data provided for population aged 15-49 are point estimates for each country. The reference year is 2007. Indicators in World and Regional Listing section provided by Population Reference Bureau 2008 World Population Data Sheet.

Demographic, social and economic indicators

Total population 2009, projected population 2050, average annual population growth rate for 2005-2010. Source: United Nations Population Division. These indicators present the size, projected future size (based on the United Nation's Population Division's medium-variant growth scenario) and current period annual growth of national populations.

Per cent urban, urban growth rates. Source: United Nations Population Division. These indicators reflect the proportion of the national population living in urban areas and the growth rate in urban areas projected.

Agricultural population per hectare of arable and permanent crop land. Source: Food and Agriculture Organization, Statistics Division, using population data based on the total populations from: United Nations Population Division. 2009. *World Population Prospects: The 2008 Revision.* New York: United Nations; and activity rates of economically active population from: International Labour Organization (ILO). 1996. *Economically Active Population, 1950-2010*, 4th Edition. Geneva: ILO. This indicator relates the size of the agricultural population to the land suitable for agricultural production. It is responsive to changes in both the structure of national economies (proportions of the workforce in agriculture) and in technologies for land development. The measure of the indicator is also responsive to different development levels and land use policies. Data refer to 2006.

Total fertility rate (2009). Source: United Nations Population Division. The measure indicates the number of children a woman would have during her reproductive years if she bore children at the rate estimated for different age groups in the specified time period. Countries may reach the projected level at different points within the period.

Births with skilled attendants. Source: WHO Database on proportion of birth by a skilled worker. Department of Reproductive Health and Research. Geneva: WHO. 2009. This indicator is based on national reports of the proportion of births attended by "skilled health personnel or skilled attendant: doctors (specialist or non-specialist) and/or persons with midwifery skills who can diagnose and manage obstetrical complications as well as normal deliveries." Data for more developed countries reflect their higher levels of skilled delivery attendance. Because of assumptions of full coverage, data (and coverage) deficits of marginalized populations and the impacts of chance and transport delays may not be fully reflected in official statistics. Data estimates are the most recent available for 2007.

Gross national income per capita. Source: Most recent (2007) figures from: The World Bank. *World Development Indicators Online.* Web site: http://devdata.worldbank.org/dataonline/ (by subscription). This indicator (formerly referred to as gross national product [GNP] per capita) measures the total output of goods and services for final use produced by residents and non-residents, regardless of allocation to domestic and foreign claims, in relation to the size of the population. As such, it is an indicator of the economic productivity of a nation. It differs from gross domestic product (GDP) by further adjusting for income received from abroad for labour and capital by residents, for similar payments to non-residents, and by incorporating various technical adjustments including those related to exchange rate changes over time. This measure also takes into account the differing purchasing power of currencies by including purchasing power parity (PPP) adjustments of "real GNP." Some PPP figures are based on regression models; others are extrapolated from the latest International Comparison Programme benchmark estimates.

Central government expenditures on education and health. Source: The World Bank. *World Development Indicators 2009* and *World Development Indicators Online* respectively. Web site: http://devdata.worldbank.org/dataonline/ (by subscription). These indicators reflect the priority afforded to education and health sectors by a country through the government expenditures dedicated to them. They are not sensitive to differences in allocations within sectors, e.g., primary education or health services in relation to other levels, which vary considerably. Direct comparability is complicated by the different administrative and budgetary responsibilities allocated to central governments in relation to local governments, and to the varying roles of the private and public sectors. Reported estimates are presented as shares of GDP per capita (for education) or total GDP (for health). Great caution is also advised

about cross-country comparisons because of varying costs of inputs in different settings and sectors. Provisional data are for the most recent year estimates available for 2007 for education and 2006 for health.

External assistance for population. Source: UNFPA. 2009. *Financial Resource Flows for Population Activities in 2007.* New York: UNFPA. These data provide the amount of external assistance expended in 2007 for population activities in each country. External funds are disbursed through multilateral and bilateral assistance agencies and by non-governmental organizations. Donor countries are indicated by their contributions being placed in parentheses. Regional totals include both country-level projects and regional activities (not otherwise reported in the table).

Under-5 mortality male/female. Source: United Nations Population Division. This indicator relates to the incidence of mortality to infants and young children. It reflects, therefore, the impact of diseases and other causes of death on infants, toddlers and young children. More standard demographic measures are infant mortality and mortality rates for 1 to 4 years of age, which reflect differing causes of and frequency of mortality in these ages. The measure is more sensitive than infant mortality to the burden of childhood diseases, including those preventable by improved nutrition and by immunization programmes. Under-5 mortality is here expressed as deaths to children under the age of 5 per 1,000 live births in a given year. Estimates are for the 2005-2010 period.

Per capita energy consumption. Source: The World Bank. *World Development Indicators Online.* Web site: http://devdata. worldbank.org/dataonline/ (by subscription). This indicator reflects annual consumption of commercial primary energy (coal, lignite, petroleum, natural gas and hydro, nuclear and geothermal electricity) in kilograms of oil equivalent per capita. It reflects the level of industrial development, the structure of the economy and patterns of consumption. Changes over time can reflect changes in the level and balance of various economic activities and changes in the efficiency of energy use (including decreases or increases in wasteful consumption). Data estimates are for 2006.

Access to improved drinking water sources. Source: WHO. 2009. Web site: http://www.who.int/whosis/ indicators/compendium/2008/2wst/(by subscription). *Meeting the MDG Drinking Water and Sanitation Target: The Urban and Rural Challenge of the Decade.* Geneva: World Health Organization. This indicator reports the percentage of the population with access to an *improved source* of drinking water providing an *adequate amount of safe water* located within a *convenient distance* from the user's dwelling. The italicized words use country-level definitions. The indicator is related to exposure to health risks, including those resulting from improper sanitation. Data are estimates for the year 2006.